Self-Discipline

Achieve Your Goals & Live the Life You Want

(How to Build your Self-Confidence, Improve your Time Management and your Emotional Intelligence)

Patrick Macleod

Published By **Phil Dawson**

Patrick Macleod

All Rights Reserved

Self-Discipline: Achieve Your Goals & Live the Life You Want (How to Build your Self-Confidence, Improve your Time Management and your Emotional Intelligence)

ISBN   978-1-998927-29-6

No part of this guidebook shall be reproduced in any form without permission in writing from the publisher except in the case of brief quotations embodied in critical articles or reviews.

Legal & Disclaimer

The information contained in this book is not designed to replace or take the place of any form of medicine or professional medical advice. The information in this book has been provided for educational & entertainment purposes only.

The information contained in this book has been compiled from sources deemed reliable, and it is accurate to the best of the Author's knowledge; however, the Author cannot guarantee its accuracy and validity and cannot be held liable for any errors or omissions. Changes are periodically made to this book. You must consult your doctor or get professional medical advice before using any of the suggested remedies, techniques, or information in this book.

Table Of Contents

Chapter 1: Using Insecurity To Build Self-Discipline

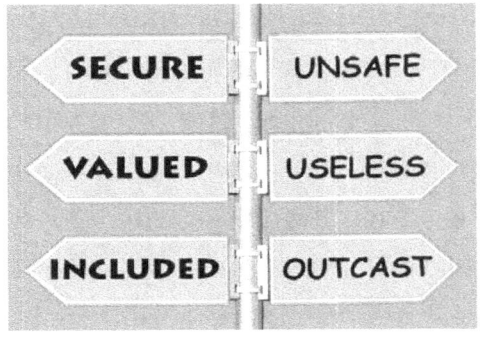

Insecurity is a loss of bear in mind or assurance. Some synonyms consist of uncertainty, precariousness, shakiness, and weakness. Vulnerability is the sensation that your mind-set and position in existence lack on top of things and do not forget. You have a willing and shaky basis in which you feature, and each person can purpose highbrow and emotional disruption. We are all fighting with lack of self warranty on some diploma. Only consider a time at the same time as you've got been feeling proper about completing a assignment. You've been tweaking and perfecting it for hours. You imagined humans marveling on the ingenuity for your imagination. And you showed a cherished one or coworker your crown jewel. They said sheepishly, "Oh, this is exceptional," with a look of disapproval and confusion. At that 2d, all you favored to do turn out to be move slowly underneath a rock. You have vowed in no way again to create anything. What do you accept as true with you studied? You did not. Such instances can be proportional to the degree you exercise self-control wherein worry has the awesome of you. After all, if no individual cares to strive new subjects, why are you purported to? And being mocked thru family, cherished ones, so strangers are difficult.

You're rational thru thinking in those phrases. What wants to be mocked for innovation and possibilities? But what is the private fee of happiness at some point of a whole life in case your insecurities strength you? And what is the effect of electricity of will on uncertainty?

The direction many human beings take is to allow uncertainty to harm their lives. You cannot most effective make bigger more strength of will by manner of being often egocentric however moreover construct a lifestyles of happiness. Progressive selfishness is the belief that you act as a version of conduct and a way of assignment desires that benefit you and society predominantly in your self-hobby. Regressive greed, on the other hand, is the belief that any individual has to lose to win. The different individual now not high-quality desires to be afflicted through manner of regressive selfishness but furthermore has to be humiliated and annihilated.

There are a few processes to apply your insecurities to construct your electricity of thoughts via innovative selfishness to turn out to be happier and extra a success.

Here are some strategies to get the approach began.

Use your fear as a universal overall performance catalyst. Psychologists postulate that the lack of some element over its income motivates people more. Anxiety can, therefore, be a motivator. You can surely be endorsed via using your worry of ridicule, guilt, disappointment, or isolation to do high-quality subjects. It has been counseled that his father and men, who knew him as a toddler, considered President John F. Kennedy as depressed and distracted. His son Joseph P. Kennedy, Jr. Is understood to have the Kennedy circle of relatives's most large promise. John have turn out to be the anointed guy after Joseph changed into killed in the Second World War to position the family inner politics. Much of the inspiration of Kennedy came from a choice to satisfaction his father (Joseph P. Kennedy, Sr.) and to prove to the area that he have to make a contribution. Use your insecurities and triumph over them as a manner to reveal the world your real rate. Although you could encounter levels of setback and disappointment, as you develop the electricity of mind to have a take a look at through on duties, yourself-self perception will increase. The massive distinction among success and failure is the capability to hold plugging away until a leap ahead takes place.

Start with and whittle it down with a popular hobby. Experts have identified the importance of ardour in the vicinity of motivation and peak overall performance for 60-plus years. Passion is, at its middle, the emotional strength that pushes ahead motion. It can be the engine if love had been part of a car. This brings you toward your goals till you integrate ardour with exercising. You will locate your cognizance becoming more unique, even though, as you bypass. With a passion for baking desserts, you will probably begin. You might also additionally then whittle down your passion for baking first-rate cakes. Later then, genuinely baking cakes of chocolate. In this way, you begin experimenting with precise varieties of chocolate as you make bigger self-control in your vicinity of facts. The down whittling approach commonly leads you to the middle of your motivation. The greater you are specific, the extra know-how to procure. This revel in builds receive as real with and respect.

Engage within the technique of strength of will. Only a records of awesome consequences is self-self notion. Winners who've conquered the challenges of lifestyles have acquired self-assurance from a very good collection. The center of gaining electricity and distinction is movement and look at-up. The key to success and happiness is the functionality to stay the route, study, and boom alongside the way, whether or not or no longer it is weight reduction, business enterprise development, or instructional plans. You ought to enjoy the concept of being inspired through the ardour you've got got got. At the time it want to be finished, normally do what is wanted. And do no longer delegate or skip over anyone else's responsibility. The willingness to self-control is one. The specific person turns into an professional with excessive self-self guarantee when you delegate your responsibilities to someone else.

That's how a person inclined to do the hobby. You're not going to thieve your thoughts.

Now you understand the decision of the sport of the usage of power of will to reveal your insecurities into achievement. You want to create a task to illustrate your rate to the sector, find out a ardour, whittle it all of the way right down to its tiny factors, and stay the course with the useful resource of the use of sticking to the system. Ultimately, you are not best going to boom strength of will and self-confidence, but you are additionally going to create a modern-day life.

Chapter 2: How To Develop Self-Discipline

Adding strength of will into your

relationships, really worth ethic, nutrients and health is needed to be glad, lead a healthful lifestyle, and achieve desires. Feelings and impulses want to now not dictate your choices. It need to be informed and rational. Of route, you can educate your self to be self-disciplined. Through exercise and repetition on your ordinary existence, you could create top behavior, dissolve terrible ones, and beautify your choice-making method. This way, you stay a lifestyles that loose and entire of wholesome picks.

Self-vicinity isn't always inborn. It is much like a muscle that toughens as you work out through the years. Here are processes to beautify your power of will.

Understand your motivation

First, in advance than you can increase energy of will, you need to have a robust desire to carry out a particular aim. A strong desire fuels energy of thoughts. Something desires to encourage that exchange. To live targeted in your route willpower, there want to be a compelling purpose why you take on a task or project.

What do you need? Why do you want it? Why exactly do you need to get it executed? What desired very last results you've got were given in thoughts? This will be a dependancy you need to expand or a cause you want to gain. The more compelling your reasons, the more potent your strength of mind.

Eliminate temptations

Your strength of will may be more potent on the same time as you follow the "out of sight, out of mind" principle. This manner doing all your feasible terrific to cast off all distractions and temptations out of your right away environment. Trying to undertake a healthful diet regime? Toss out the junk meals for your fridge. Want to turn out to be greater targeted while analyzing? Switch off your phone!

Adopt a wholesome and regular food plan

Scientists have decided that your resolve lessens whenever your blood sugar is low. When you're hungry, your capability to pay attention is impeded because your mind isn't on foot at its maximum ability. Hunger no longer simplest reduces interest; it additionally drives pessimism and grouchiness. A terrible food regimen will have an impact in your energy of will in all factors of your life—from relationships to work. With healthful and normal food, however, your blood sugar degree is regulated, and your consciousness and decision-making abilities are more ideal.

Do it regardless of the reality that doesn't sense "proper"

To enhance your strength of mind, you need to be organized to change your regular normal. This is regularly tough and painful for plenty of us. The hassle is, our dependancy behaviors are connected to the basal ganglia (a part of the thoughts answerable for reminiscences, patterns, and emotions). However, our choices are related to a separate place of the thoughts called the prefrontal cortex. When a behavior will become a dependancy, we go automobile-pilot and prevent the use of our choice-making abilities. So, to interrupt a awful addiction and construct a current day one, you need to make active choices; this approach regularly feels wrong due to the fact the mind will combat the trade and stay with what it is been programmed to perform. This is why you need to make active picks even at the same time as you don't revel in find it impossible to resist.

Procrastination plays a first rate position proper proper here. Self-subject says: do it now! While a reprieve is good, embracing procrastination approach sinking deeper into stagnation. Channel your strength into what subjects the most and hold anchoring yourself in your purpose.

Create an action plan

To collect your purpose, you want to create an effective movement plan. This plan have to include mini-milestones and an much less pricey cut-off date. Mini-milestones assist you splitting your purpose into practicable chunks—moving within the route of your purpose in small quantities at a time. This manner, you stay on top of factors of the purpose, and you aren't crushed. By taking one step at a time, you simplify the process and begin to assemble momentum.

An crushed thoughts without hassle procrastinates. And procrastination is a number one stumbling block to power of thoughts. Therefore, your movement plan want to have modern steps and small wins as you thing in the direction of your purpose.

A reduce-off date offers a revel in of urgency and focus. Your route to self-discipline must have a realistic last date. A easy reduce-off date disciplines your recognition. When there may be a particular stop-date, your strength and property are as it ought to be used in retaining the preferred momentum to take a look at via together with your moves.

Have a self-disciplined mind-set

Your usa of thoughts is installed on your strength of will. There are particular traits— consisting of optimism, braveness, enthusiasm, delight, passion, diligence, ardour, endurance, and diligence— you have to imbibe. You need to be devoted to performing some aspect is crucial to reap your motive. You want to be prepared to revel in the manner and make it a part of you.

Likewise, a self-disciplined thoughts knows the essence of priorities. A disciplined lifestyles is all about flow and structure. By focusing on the most critical issue, you are a good deal much less possibly to get sidetracked with beside the aspect stuff.

Visualize your desired effects

Being self-disciplined in a unmarried specific component of your lifestyles is the goal. Keep visualizing that preferred very last outcomes. This gives more readability about your dreams and the actions wished to carry out them. After you have got have been given defined your desires, believe how you'll feel in relation to fruition. There is strength in visualization and imagination. By developing a mental photograph of your purpose, you have were given taken step one in the direction of making it palpable.

Note that visualization isn't similar to having a pipe dream. Visualization is constructed upon specific and mentioned goals. A daydreamer best fantasizes with out lifting a finger inside the course of any plan. When you visualize, get rid of all self-doubt. To be self-disciplined, you want to learn how to pass head-on, leaving no region for terrible thoughts to crawl into your subconscious.

Monitor your improvement

Appreciate each improvement you are making inside the course of your purpose. Whether you are the usage of a journal or calendar, tune each development, and degree your boom. This will hold you focused and encouraged as you attain your milestones. And even while you fail to achieve a milestone, tracking your development permits you notice the modifications you want to install vicinity to get lower back in the sport and the pitfalls you want to cast off. These pitfalls are regularly natural. The most critical hassle is studying from them and moving beforehand.

Find out the feasible roadblocks and demanding situations that could pop up along the path to strength of mind. Take beneath attention your weaknesses and dedicate time in sprucing the talents wished to overcome those lacking areas.

Be responsible and devoted

You want an unwavering willpower to perform any cause. Long-time period self-control powers strength of mind. But due to the reality there may be regularly no duty, we brief lose determination.

Accountability is a focus of energy of will. For extended-time period strength of will, you want someone to hold you accountable for your movements. A buddy, member of the family, mentor, or maybe a health teacher. Someone straightforward checking in on you to assess your development. This second motivating voice goes an extended way in helping you acquire your desires.

You need to moreover be chargeable for your necessities. Something to keep your right away on the same time as you move off beam. As you locate someone to hold you accountable, you need to moreover preserve yourself accountable for your normal selections and alternatives.

Also, look out for position models (circle of relatives, pals, and co-personnel) who have previously carried out the goal you desire. From coaches to professors to even colleagues, many human beings are higher and extra experienced than you're. These are human beings who have lengthy long past thru your modern-day-day state of affairs. Rather than stumbling approximately inside the darkish, toying with trials and errors, there can be no damage in soliciting for assist and course. Using their enjoy and gaining knowledge of how they located thru with high-quality actions that had been given them the ones goals, you may paintings electricity of will into your non-public journey. A supportive environment is critical. New conduct are without problems formed if you have human beings to preserve your devoted, stimulated and focused.

Commitment fuels willpower. No remember what worrying situations lies in advance, you need to organized to paste on your purpose. One trouble I honestly have determined useful is to make a public willpower. For example, I told severa family participants, pals, own family contributors and colleagues approximately my plans to prevent smoking. This manner, I come to be held more chargeable for my moves and I modified into helped to live disciplined alongside my non-smoking adventure.

But commitment is in no way about your final goal. You need to be devoted to every step that might reason that purpose. To keep away from smoking, for instance, I did now not just flow bloodless turkey. I had to be devoted to preventing gatherings that would set off to smoke; I needed to attend Nicotine Anonymous conferences, use NRTs, and so on. Committing to little moves way being consistent with many behavior that could culminate yours inside the final aim. This manner, you can avoid getting sidetracked sucked into the lure of immediately gratification.

Be forgiving of yourself

Self-field is tough. There can be up and downs. The most essential element is to hold attempting. Acknowledge your setback and pass in advance. Instead of lingering in frustration, anger, or guilt because of the reality you slipped once more right proper into a awful addiction, forgive yourself and get back in the sport. The longer you mourn your failure, the tougher it turns into to get back heading within the right course.

That little voice internal your head, the handiest that constantly reminds you of the negatives, is capable of dragging you right right down to the gutters. Most instances, we're our personal enemies on our route to willpower. We located ourselves down and count on we are able to in no way be accurate enough.

Learn to forgive yourself. As easy because it sounds, forgiving oneself is one of the toughest topics there is. But it's the maximum crucial. Understand that no character is right. We all have our insecurities. But lifestyles needs no longer to be first-rate for people to be happy about themselves. There is a distinctive feature in reputation, taking walks to be better, and contentment.

Avoid the entice of perfectionism

Perfectionism is a self-sabotaging stress. Perfectionism tips us into questioning we are truly making development. Perfectionism, inside the real feel, is a protective mechanism that shields us from doing the real artwork. To see excellent, we cognizance at the trivial responsibilities that deliver us some semblance of manipulate; Thereby, we hold fooling ourselves into questioning we're exercise electricity of will.

Expecting lots from yourself is a extremely good aspect, but perfectionism will have a paralyzing effect if no longer nicely treated—a roadblock closer to your development and achievements.

While, on the surface, being a perfectionist sounds tremendous: you've got a keen eye for facts, generally seeking to surpass expectations and focused on the subsequent massive hassle. However, there are various methods wherein perfectionism can serve a roadblock for you.

When you attempt for perfectionism, you can turn out to be procrastinating about the dreams you are even passionate about. Because you spend numerous time conjuring the right vision of the manner subjects need to be performed, you switch out to be overly element-oriented and obsess about every issue. Soon, because of the fact it's far painful expending too much energy on that mission, you push it away and look forward to that "great" 2nd—which can also in no manner come.

Another hassle with perfectionists is the trouble of skewed reality. Because thru putting a excessive private giant for perfection, they have a tendency to expect more than what's realistic. Because they hold difficult themselves physically and emotionally to accumulate that "quality" very last effects, they come to be lacking the massive photo because of their huge self-expectancies.

There is a deep disappointment that plagues maximum perfectionists. The preference for precision can create feelings of distress every day. Anxiety will generally arise even as you hold obsessing over the outcome of a goal or whilst you maintain beating your self up approximately a slip-up. You in the end turn out to be disenchanted and trapped, regretting even the smallest of factors. In specific terms, perfectionists will be predisposed to maintain stopping despair, wondering their self confidence based totally on their output and ordinary basic overall performance.

When you are normally striving for perfection, there may be a threat which you are brushing off your health inside the call of sporting out the proper stop end result. To beat a lessen-off date or adopt a addiction, you exercise self-neglect about, allowing your fitness to fail over time.

Finally, perfectionism can bring about compromised relationships. A perfectionist may additionally positioned artwork above his or her cherished ones and may be over-annoying of them as well. Perfectionists also are at risk of lash out whilst topics do no longer drift their way. To conquer the roadblocks of perfectionism, consider focusing on what truely topics on your existence, save you defining your self esteem through manner of using a listing of accomplishments, and notice errors as a chance to have a take a look at.

Chapter 3: Importance Of A Correct Lifestyle And Nutrition

Among the first-rate versions in our lives is the meals wherein we devour. A lot of Americans do no longer eat a healthful food regimen, and greater than an low cost share is obese. Lots of physicians assume that pressure and the onslaught of people suffering with melancholy are due to a nutrients scarcity. The strain that a number of us experience nowadays might be the very last outcomes of actually not ingesting a healthy diet regime.

All parents apprehend that suitable vitamins is important for a healthy frame;

however, what about a healthful thoughts? We pay attention greater about an remarkable food regimen for mental health in addition to bodily fitness.

Particular meals are natural temper enhancers. These encompass:

•Dairy merchandise. Dairy is typically immoderate in protein and may decorate a physical response to strain. You can take dairy in milk or cheese and expect a lot less bodily issues because of stress similarly to taking satisfaction in a lighter mood;

•Fish. Fish this is full-size in fat, collectively with salmon, blessings the frame along aspect the thoughts. All people recognize that fish is considered as mind food, however fish this is excessive in Omega-3 fats is a natural manner to deal with despair. Some research endorse that people who revel in depression related to strain have low ranges of Omega-3 fat inside their frame;

•Turkey. It is every other food to be able to boom serotonin. Turkey includes Tryptophan, an amino acid which could honestly make you lighten up. Keep in mind how worn-out you felt after eating Thanksgiving supper ultimate 12 months? That emerge as from the Tryptophan, a herbal tranquilizer;

•Brazil Nuts. These encompass selenium, it is a few other temper enhancer. Nevertheless, too much of this can prove dangerous to your gadget so ensure to consume these nuts pretty.

•Complex carbs. These likewise encompass tryptophan and, even though we've got had been given truely been cautioned to avoid carbohydrates those past couples of years, we require complex carbohydrates, now not clean carbs.

If you are not getting enough of those elements on your everyday healthy eating plan, reflect onconsideration on taking a multivitamin or a supplement. If you are experiencing strain, the percentages are that you may lack vitamins B along side Omega-3 acids.

Eating the precise healthy dietweight-reduction plan definitely won't hurt you and might in reality wind up eliminating a first-rate deal of your stress.

Exercise is, likewise, essential to doing away with stress. As a depend of truth, at the equal time as you enjoy pressure starting, the very brilliant trouble that you can do to stave it off is to training session. Doing a few thing bodily can often in fact exercising the trouble that you are having.

Cardio carrying events are the very high-quality method to exercising stress. These get your coronary coronary coronary heart pumping and truly boom the serotonin to your mind, setting you in a miles higher state of thoughts. Stress can be extremely straining on your bodily being, and exercise can right the incorrect and get your body again into scenario. Exercise likewise will boom the body's immune gadget, which additionally struggles with strain.

Get your self into an exercising routine. Exercise within the morning or after art work doing cardiovascular bodily sports on the manner to offer every your body and mind an increase, at the facet of help handling pressure. At night time time, you may exercising yoga or stretching wearing occasions which can assist with toning your frame in addition to loosen up you.

Do not desire to exercising consultation? Do a few element physical. Cleaning up the kitchen vicinity floor will now not simply ease your strain. It will, likewise, get the floor in fact tidy. Doing a few aspect physical in conjunction with cleansing, is some of the very brilliant stress reducers obtainable. It works a splendid deal better than any pill, prices no longer some component, and, on the same time as you are completed, you may have a absolutely tidy home.

Chapter 4: Importance Of Sleeping Well

Sleeping well and regularly has a number of advantages. Some of them are:

1.Reduce pressure and blood stress

When you get an notable night time's sleep after a hectic day, it serves as a launch that calms your nerves. Your body remains in a regular usa of calm relaxation that lowers your blood stress and reduces strain and anxiety.

2.Improves your intellectual health

Getting a wholesome dose of sleep may be very beneficial to our intellectual health.

Studies have proven that at the same time as you sleep properly and regularly;

i.it improves your reminiscence,

ii.it improves your ability to expect significantly and resolve problems,

iii.it locations your thoughts inside the right frame to select up new records effects,

iv. it lets in you control your emotions better,

v.it reduces the threat of mood swings and depression

three.Sleep can help manage your appetite

A study finished showed that folks who are sleep deprived are more likely to eat more than individuals who get sufficient sleep. The motive within the decrease back of this finding is that once we sleep, our frame secretes greater ghrelin — a hormone that stimulates appetite, thereby inflicting us to devour extra. So in case you are searching your weight, you shouldn't deprive your body of a notable night time's sleep.

four.Sleep facilitates your body rejuvenate

It has; it's that sleep permits restore our immune tool. A study finished showed that parents that are sleep deprived are more vulnerable to contaminating infections that those with a healthy sleep pattern.

five.Sleep help lessen pain

Have you observed that any time you nod off with a minor harm, you wake up feeling a whole lot an awful lot much less ache than you probable did the night time in advance than? Several studies has confirmed that sleep lets in our body heal quicker than it might if you have been aware and physical lively.

Sleep a accurate widespread shape of hours

The body enjoys a habitual. It thrives on dependancy. With a everyday bedtime and wake-up time, your body is extra possibly to stay heading within the proper path. If you can, avoid numerous schedules, late-night time time activities, night time shifts, or other topics that could intrude along aspect your sleep ordinary.

When you have got a hard time falling asleep, try to drink a glass of heat milk, it's far a conventional answer for insomnia, and there's evidence that it could will permit you to get advanced extremely good of sleep. Not handiest does milk assist prevent hunger from troubling your sleep, however it moreover contains an amino acid known as tryptophan, that is converted within the mind proper right into a peaceful chemical known as serotonin. Calcium can be very pro-metabolic, lowering strain and lowering levels of parathyroid hormone, which has been recounted to contribute to insomnia.

Not simply that, you can constantly alter your personal day by day routine to comprise time for yoga or meditation. There is a wealth of proof that yoga and meditation can beautify sleep styles, regularly significantly. Having some amusement time for your self is critical. These strategies can be completed at domestic for each consolation and privacy.

It lets in to beautify the overall flexibility of your frame, unwind your thoughts, and destress your body. Attempt to spend not less than half of-hour an afternoon to both meditate or do yoga. Generally, meditation and yoga are fine completed inside the morning, in a non violent place and with exposure to daytime.

For meditation, all you want to carry out is sit down down down and empty your mind. Attempt to take note of enjoyable song to assist quiet you down. The second you start to get used to the concept of meditating in some unspecified time in the destiny of the day, the thoughts will control to lighten up faster at night time time, and for this reason, you will have an much less tough time going to sleep. As for yoga, you can each select yoga commands with numerous pals or exercise at domestic for additonal solitude. It will assist you sleep in masses of techniques. The exercising of particular yoga postures will improve the blood glide to the sleep middle in the mind, which has the effect of normalizing the sleep cycle. Keep in thoughts; sleep isn't always a lifestyle option or a pricey; it's miles herbal and required. So root out the governing motives, alter your food plan, drink a tumbler of warm milk, establish a sound asleep time desk, do some yoga and meditate. Follow the quantities of the recommendation talked about above, and always, you will get your top notch sleep.

It's hard to deal with insomnia when you have no power left in the back of internal you. You'll constantly feel worn-out and care less approximately matters which is probably taking location round you. Your thoughts will stray, and frequently the ones mind don't make any experience. Life itself is currently complicated sufficient. Now, believe which consist of the reality that you are not receiving any relaxation and need to address every mission lifestyles gives you. How could you experience? Bewildered? Worried?

You may also become losing time at your place of job. You might possibly fall quick to prepare your own family dishes and dissatisfied your kids. You can also start forgetting about all of the small matters that you normally do for your intimate relationship. Many regions in your existence can skip south due to insomnia. With these forms of in thoughts, now might be the time to guard yourself from losing sleep and get a first-rate rest each night time.

Although now not all insomnia is brought about through stress, it's miles indisputable that folks that come across ongoing stress are greater vulnerable to insomnia. When it involves stress-related insomnia, treating, or doing away with the stress will reduce insomnia. As referred to in the earlier financial ruin of this ebook, pressure affects the terrific of 1's sleep, which can disturb his or her sleep rhythm. Thus, one will discover it hard to drop off to sleep at night time time time and live awake at a few degree within the day.

It is vital to cope with all areas of your lifestyles within the pleasant way possible to look to it that you are at a healthful balance. You want to ensure which you have become correct sufficient sleep on an everyday basis. Sleep plays a large position for your physical fitness. Inadequate sleep for a quick time may additionally furthermore make you more irritable and quick-tempered. Long-time period affects may be large: cardiac troubles, depression, stroke, coronary coronary coronary heart assault, among others.

According to sleep experts, numerous research observed out that once human beings get exact enough sleep, they will no longer without a doubt experience better, however may also moreover boom their probabilities of living longer, more healthy, and extra fulfilled lives.

To conquer insomnia, you have to keep away from any nicotine, caffeine, and alcohol. All of those will reason the thoughts to grow to be uneasy over time absolutely. Having a non-forestall quantity of caffeine will compel the mind to be greater energetic than it's miles.

Most humans require the electricity to begin their day, so that they select out out stimulants. Caffeine is the diverse maximum well-known alternatives of stimulants these days to guarantee alertness and wakefulness within the morning and for the the relaxation of the day. However, they're oblivious to the reality that caffeine is most of the top motives of insomnia. It messes up the natural stability of wakefulness and sleep.

Therefore, insomniacs have to keep away from those drinks to have exquisite sleep. Miss that espresso harm, attain for a glass of normal water in choice to the coffee, which may be the cause why you are having trouble falling and closing asleep at some stage in the night time time time.

Besides that, putting in a nap routine for yourself is a number of the top notch self-help strategies for insomnia. It is a superb sized step in conquering insomnia for particular. It is so vital to go to mattress at the identical time at night time time and stand up the identical time every morning because of the fact the frame calls for consistency.

Chapter 5: Positive Mindset

Existing within our minds are some of specific subsystems that art work collectively to show up our mind and moves. Some of those subsystems normally exist under our popularity, and others often input into recognition.

These subsystems have their pastimes and motivations. They perform as man or woman entities. Your subsystems aren't continually strolling in the direction of the same targets as you, but they aren't normally in the direction of you every.

Just like actual humans in a actual corporation, your subsystems alternate their minds, have relationships with each exceptional, and turn out to be extra or an entire lot plenty less influential on any given day. There are some subsystems that everyone has, and there are some subsystems which might be precise to you. Here is a listing of some of the equal old subsystems you are likely to locate to your mind.

The Dopamine Reward Pathway

In 1954, Olds and Milner, researchers at McGill University, posted a groundbreaking paper on the praise center inside the mind. They set up electrodes to the septal region of rats' brains and gave the ones rats the functionality to stimulate themselves thru an electric powered shock through pressing a pedal. Some unique experiments found out that the rats may additionally do nearly anything to stimulate themselves. They should overlook ingesting despite manifestly being hungry, and they were inclined to go through harsh bodily ache (walk on a in fact painful electrified floor) as a manner to receive a marvel.

Researchers in this era have been doing a whole lot of experiments at the praise-punishment device in rats, however inside the past, they'd used food and water as rewards. With food and water, the reward impact might prevent taking walks after the rats had end up satiated, however with the direct mind stimulation, the rats never have become satiated and could maintain to press the pedal for hours on quit. The researchers concluded that they must have discovered a delight middle inside the thoughts.

It didn't take prolonged for this equal check to be completed on human beings. Dr. Heath at the University of Tulane in Louisiana surgically implanted electrodes into the reward pathway in human beings's brains and gave them the functionality to stimulate themselves using a switch. The patients ought to stimulate themselves without a result in sight deciding on not to consume however understanding that they've been hungry, and one of the patients became irate when advocated that it became time to disconnect the electrodes. Probably this take a look at wouldn't be authorized with the beneficial aid of ethics boards these days, but understanding the studies continues to be useful. Interviews with human patients gave us some specially illuminating records.

The electric powered shocks didn't bring about natural delight; in truth, the various sufferers professional a combination of exceptional and terrible feelings. For example, one affected person professional tension because of the fact he felt like he grow to be drawing near bliss with the resource of beautiful himself, but couldn't quite get there no matter how hard he tried.

The outcomes of these interviews are ordinary with the Buddhist idea this is attempting reasons struggling. The contributors within the study expert a superb diploma of suffering because of their preference for a more transcendent degree of pleasure which the shocks couldn't offer.

Ordinary activities and gadgets in ordinary lifestyles, which incorporates luxurious products, addictive pills, junk food, and social media, stimulate dopamine in a similar way. Interestingly, just like the electrical shocks on this observe, these sorts of gadgets produce each superb and bad emotions as nicely.

There is a sturdy strength towards eating or shopping for the ones devices, but this doesn't propose that they certainly make you revel in right as an entire. Sure, you can anticipate you want to eat an entire discipline of doughnuts inside the parking zone, but the imagined pleasure of giving in to this choice is a lot higher than the actual pride of giving in. Not to say all the terrible emotions that can end end result from consuming a whole container of doughnuts inside the parking lot (shame, stomach ache, lethargy, and so forth.).

The dopamine reward pathway is an vital and influential subsystem in our minds. Its interest is to guide our behavior through praise or contrarily, to guide our behavior via the absence of praise, that is successfully punishment.

The Buddhist idea of Nirvana is to obtain a rustic in that you've were given transcended your dopamine praise device and aren't beholden to its whims. Although this is an appealing answer, it isn't the recommendation given on this ebook. Instead, the opportunity is to mix the dopamine reward machine right right into a rational practical unified series of subsystems.

The dopamine reward pathway may be extraordinarily influential in our behavior. It is crucial to recognize its have an impact on, mood this have an impact on while it is faulty, and take advantage of the have an impact on even as it's miles pointing us within the right route.

Earlier we referred to how the dopamine praise pathway encourages us to do all sorts of nasty things like eating junk food or using addictive pills, but it may furthermore make us do topics which are in our hobby as nicely, consisting of going to the gymnasium, showing up for art work, or working toward an device. In reality, the bulk of our behavior is in a few way mediated through using the dopamine reward tool.

If you are feeling a strong inclination inside the direction of behavior that is on your excellent interest in the lengthy-run, then use that momentum and allow your dopaminergic pathway to guide your behaviour. However, in case you are feeling a sturdy inclination inside the path of a terrible conduct use the guidelines within the segment on Resistance to Temptation: emerge as aware of the choice, apprehend that giving in received't deliver you any form of lasting or transcendent happiness, and then allow the selection cross rather than try to fight it.

Chapter 6: The Power Of Positive Addiction

If you observe how addiction works... it starts offevolved offevolved small and regularly leads you to an increasing number of. How are we able to get an animal to obey our commands? We lead it and deliver little treats alongside the way. You never offer it a cope with large enough to meet it surely. People grow to be addicted to tablets with the resource of taking it in small portions and regularly developing the frequency. If a person is given a large dose of drugs proper on the begin, it may probably be lethal. When you drink alcohol, there may be no massive reward on the give up. The very last result of eating isn't a few element you crave: hangover, headache, vomit. The essential enchantment of alcohol is the feeling which you get on the equal time as consuming. That's what the mind cares approximately – the manner you experience in the period in-between?

That's why it's miles crucial to ensure that the prevent praise logically is useful to you. It's going to provide achievement, extra income, better fitness, and topics of that nature. Your mind is in no way stimulated to get legitimate rewards. That is never going to paintings. It in no way works for every person. That's why so few human beings can do what they consciously want to do.

There's any other wonderful purpose why human beings can't try this as properly. A lot of human beings want to offer themselves a pat inside the again as early as feasible. That is a mistake. If an addiction gave you the entirety you want right at the begin, you save you doing it. Think approximately it. Have you ever finished some factor in which all the rewards had been given to you on the start, how did you feel? You possibly out of place hobby without a doubt speedy. Anything which gives you with all the rewards with the number one hour, you lose interest and begin seeking out something else. But what maximum people do, as quickly as they start a enterprise, or begin studying, or begin going to the health club, they start speakme about it to their friends, colleagues, own family individuals. They toot their very very personal horn hard. Why do people try this?

Because that's how we generate price in our head. When you speak about your success, or you start a present day business enterprise to get feelings of gratification, you gave your self a pat within the once more too early. You gave yourself all the rewards, proper at the begin. Let's accept as true with a hypothetical situation wherein I get on social media, and all of us at once gave me all of the approval I need, I might save you and look for some aspect else to do. The give up goal is anti-climactic as a ways as our dopamine loving mind is involved. So we need to do the alternative. In order to get dopamine and use it to direct our behavior, we want to provide ourselves little hits. We can in no manner allow the mind anticipate we have were given reached the end purpose.

If you have got a have a look at an in advance test accomplished on rats, each time dopamine is launched, it is brought about through the activity being achieved on the winning second. It is in no way due to attaining the purpose. It is due to the mind questioning that you are making development within the course of a reason on the manner to decorate our chances of survival. The critical dopamine launch triggers are survival and passing the genes.

These are the big ones. Things, like heading off irritating conditions and constructing safety & safety around you, triggers a dopamine release as nicely. Why? Because the ones objects help you still exist longer. So we are going to reputation on growing our social value, as a manner to growth our opportunities of survival and passing our genes. Going again to the rat check, dopamine is the most robust motivator that gets us to do some thing. It is so effective that it may make rats electrocute themselves to get it.

And as dopamine is caused with the aid of the mind being tricked into wondering it's far heading toward an goal so that it will boom our survival opportunities, our exquisite choice to take it below our control is through the usage of gambling with the VALUE. Cause price has an immediate effect on survival possibilities. So we want to discover all of the matters that have an effect on our rate or make us see ourselves in a higher value. To do that, we are able to perform a little matters.

Joining a network of human beings in which you could compete with others. One of the primary motives I preferred to benefit fulfillment as quickly as I had been given into the commercial enterprise is that I preferred to have a higher function in my network. When I first got into this, I have become now not doing nicely. Everyone left out me, said they will be busy. I endorsed the hell with the ones human beings. I preferred to reveal them wrong. I labored difficult on my enterprise employer so I can beat them. After I did that, some thing else grabbed my hobby. I joined the advertising network and began competing with different marketers. I preferred to be better than them.

Whenever we communicate approximately "I am going to be the

great", it refers to an increase in social price. On the floor, all of this doesn't make masses feel. But they make perfect experience on the same time as you have got a examine dependancy, dopamine, and the emotional brain. Logically, it would seem silly. But as you can see, dopamine controls our conduct subconsciously. It makes us do loopy subjects.

So you need to growth your fee. You want to see your self making development. For example, golfers see themselves getting better every day. In exceptional terms, their value is rising. Filmmakers get into the filmmaking corporation. As they get better at making movies, they get extra reputation. They advantage extra social benefits. They develop.

You need to find a way to boom your belief of self-worth. You want to enhance how properly you are being portrayed.

When you first get started out, don't connect your charge to big portions of cash or whatever this is too an extended way out of acquire, like winning your first chess championship or getting 1,000,000 dollars in income. You ought to link your fee to creating development and growing your capabilities and moreover evaluating your talents to unique people for your network.

Another component you may do is to play with survival. Remember, survival is the most powerful motivator inside the worldwide. Try to burn your bridges a bit. Put yourself in a particularly hard scenario wherein topics are not cushty. For example, try to placed your self in a scenario wherein you aren't snug financially. You need a bit of hassle. Difficult conditions motive survival mode, that's the simplest type of motivation you'll ever enjoy.

If you combine this with the need to compete and emerge as higher than others, you'll have a loopy effective motivation. Here's a beneficial workout that you could do: Picture your self or the people you're competing with viewing you at a better recognition degree. It sounds so regular, however take into account having that success, having all that praise, being at the pinnacle. That's going to make you crave improvement. You want to be modern and reflect onconsideration on the entirety that might increase your fee and tie it for your purpose. Give yourself little treats, little rewards alongside the way. Never supply yourself the huge cope with in advance than undertaking the quit purpose otherwise you'll emerge as glad and therefore, lose all interest.

Never go on social media and kind how a success you are. Never communicate about all your achievements and the top notch subjects you've got accomplished, and some issue that you are presently doing. Never exit there and get obsessed with a great begin. You want to offer yourself small rewards which is probably clean to accumulate proper away. Like at the same time as you release your first product, don't make a goal of attaining $100k in earnings. Your primary motive want to be getting the product on sale.

The worst issue is to declare victory after one or two income. I even have visible such a number of organisation owners do this. They throw a large birthday party due to the reality they've got reached $250 a day. They will do some thing for an early birthday party. You want to keep your self from early delight, and supply yourself little hits of dopamine constantly. You want to diploma your development inside the route of your intention. Tell yourself, "I were given a bit better at this. I were given a piece better at that. I have been given a piece bit better at email advertising and marketing. I have been given a touch bit better at – studying, art work, workout, meditation – some thing you're pursuing. It is easy to song your development at these things. But in case you personal a business, then it isn't so easy. You actually need to start recording your development. You need to degree your increase each single day. I am normally tracking the increase of my company and each time I view it, it feels wonderful. You could in all likelihood want to try this too. Don't supply your self a massive pat at the returned at the primary day. If you do, you will lose your interest. It's pretty easy in commercial employer. It's so easy to transport and sing praises approximately how high-quality you're and the topics you possibly did. So many people who initial success bypass and open Champaign and talk approximately how cool they are.

I simply have completed it too. And what came about is that I lost motivation to keep operating. I didn't have any lucrative goal to get to. So, I had to discover a totally new shape of motivation.

I had to be a part of my dopamine to my goal. You can be a part of as many physical dopamine hits to your intention as feasible. For instance, my place of business gives me a large enhance of dopamine because of the truth I meditate and drink inexperienced tea as soon as I get to my place of job. My place of business is pretty well organized. I certainly have prepared the whole lot for my flavor. I truly have lighting fixtures in keeping with my liking. I without a doubt have a specific smell in my workplace that I really like. You need your place of work to make you experience particular. You need the whole thing about your purpose to give you a dopamine boom. I even have seen workplaces of a number of entrepreneurs in which everything appears tousled. Very cluttered and disorganized. All the alternative rooms are super & tidy however their place of work looks as if a warzone. It's hard. There is trash all around. It simply appears terrible. You need each little difficulty to enjoy actual. You need to motive dopamine as you enter your workplace or any area in which you could get subjects finished.

The maximum extraordinary recommendation I have to come up with is that don't offer yourself all of the rewards proper now. Join a community that permits you to compete with distinct people for recognition and social charge. For example, at the same time as you take a look at entrepreneurs, they don't get suitable at a agency best for themselves. They want to show off a piece, specially on line. They need to move and show special humans their exceptional accomplishments because it will growth their social price. If you be a part of that feeling to something you are doing, you're going to sense especially inspired. Also, music your development and don't offer yourself the huge prize right away. It'll will permit you to expand faster and tap into that countless energy of your emotional thoughts that is added on and directed via dopamine in area of depending handiest on self-discipline which runs out speedy. If you are involved that every one of this stuff isn't going to offer you large sufficient dopamine hit, your thoughts is overstimulated. So, put off the topics which bombard your thoughts with on the spot gratification like alcohol, sugar, social media, drugs, video video games, TV. I even have determined the satisfactory manner to remove immediately gratification matters from your lifestyles is to break them.

However, it's far complex and requires an entire lot of power of will. For example, for me to restore my deleted social media profiles, I want to create new money owed on Facebook, Instagram, and unique social media web web sites, fill out my profile, look for humans to befriend or comply with, upload images, and do the whole lot else from the very starting. It will take massive attempt and self-discipline. I am not doing that. It is long gone. It's smooth for me no longer to remember social media anymore.

On the alternative issue, my place of job and laptop are flawlessly set up. I am already in work-associated agencies. I even have my organisation with me. I even have all my clients. It's very easy for me to get a dopamine release from jogging on my commercial organisation.

The ultimate detail I want to go away you with is that your dopamine triggers are going to own your thoughts all day extended. For instance, once I am on a spoil, and I am binge-looking TV indicates or going loopy on social media, I word that my thoughts are going to get ate up with TV suggests & social media. When I am chatting on Facebook, I am clearly immersed in that. And once I sign off and doze off, I am although considering what occurred in the course of the chat and what should I say the following day. Again, silly and a waste of my time. In truth, I is probably benefitted with the useful resource of considering my company, what do I want to artwork on because of the fact I am receiving coins, clients, achievement, and pleasure from walking on my enterprise. It's the first-class possibility. It's in which the advantages are in my lifestyles. But I gained't try this due to the fact dopamine release is right right here on Facebook, alcohol, and Netflix. And the maximum important hassle this is going to maintain you decrease back in lifestyles and break your development is having those immediate gratification sports activities on your life. It's going to dominate your thoughts. If you spend 4 hours in a day thinking about what is presently going inside the Game of Thrones, then the ones four hours are not going into your company.

So you can want to find out a manner to connect your dopamine triggers into your thoughts. If you have got some of ways to get instant gratification like in case you surely revel in alcohol, YouTube, smoking, doing all types of clean dopamine launch sports, the ones are going to dominate your thoughts. And that's going to bring about you now not getting proper to your craft. You acquired't get accurate for your commercial corporation. You won't get precise at your studies. You acquired't get particular in any skill which you are mastering. So that's why it is so crucial which you need to take away all property of instant gratification out of your existence. Eliminate sugar & fatty additives, dispose of the alcohol, and surrender social media. It is okay in case you do those items in the path of the damage or excursion. For instance, I watch my preferred TV shows and pass party with my buddies to sincerely forget about about work. And the ones gadgets will be predisposed to be pretty effective at that. And in my thoughts, I recognize if I am going to get decrease returned into my normal paintings time table and regain my pinnacle overall performance diploma, I need to dispose of all the ones distractions from my life. I need to make it enormously difficult for me to do those subjects. So my easygoing thoughts starts offevolved searching out fee in exclusive subjects.

Chapter 7: How To Control Pain

Pain Tolerance is area in its most primitive shape. This is the ability to stand up to physical pain within the pursuit of a intention. Pain tolerance, as a cause in itself, may also additionally rub a few human beings the incorrect way. However, ache tolerance is just one of the many critical programs of the location.

Overcoming ache is crucial while you start a cutting-edge physical pursuit. For example, if you begin strolling every day after in no way having been a everyday runner within the beyond, you will enjoy ache for your legs, feet, lungs, and likely one-of-a-kind additives of your body. As your frame and involved device adapt, you may enlarge bodily and highbrow calluses allowing you to run with out experiencing heaps pain the least bit.

With a few physical pastimes, you could commonly prompt a nation of pain through approach of really pushing your self to the restriction, even the nice lengthy-distance runners within the worldwide enjoy a few diploma of ache once they skip for a non-public document.

For many significantly disciplined humans, ache tolerance isn't always a specially important shape of region. Once they gain a essential degree of health, there may be no purpose to push themselves any in addition. Maintaining that primary fitness is not a rely of ache tolerance, but rather, it stressful situations their tolerance for boredom.

Other humans are specifically drawn to the purity of ache tolerance as a way of exercise and expressing their challenge. Vulnerability, for example, is once in a while ambiguous and can't be measured in the equal way as ache tolerance. Pain tolerance is easy, and for some humans, it's miles a greater dependable way to find this means that than some other shape of situation.

You will apprehend that pain is ready to supply a knockout blow at the same time as it convinces you that the terrible sensations you are feeling are so powerful that you can not conquer them. This is a trick, recognize what pain is trying to do, and take away its strength.

In order to conquer ache, without a doubt apprehend pain for what it's miles, a sign that a specific a part of your body is experiencing stress. Recognize pain as a experience, recognize that pain exists however select now not to recognize it as a terrible enjoy.

If you've got been triumph over thru the use of pain, so as to probably arise in the end, don't allow this failure broaden proper right into a powerful momentum. Instead, speedy make bigger momentum inside the contrary path. If the least bit feasible, move decrease decrease lower back and do the interest once more, however this time follow thru to the surrender. Sometimes it's miles not possible or volatile to redo an interest. If this is the case, discover each one-of-a-kind technique to get lower returned at the disciplined course, whether or not or no longer this is overcoming ache or strengthening a few one-of-a-type form of power of will.

Just like maximum terrible emotions, pain isn't continuously vestigial; in a few times, it's miles virtually presenting you with treasured information. Occasionally, a painful sign manner which you are injured, ill, or are approximately to injure your self. In this example, you need to concentrate to the ache and go into reverse.

This is wherein self-knowledge comes into play; it may be tough to understand the difference amongst giving up unnecessarily and the usage of suitable caution. The greater experience you have had been given with exercise your pain tolerance, the extra powerful you will be at reading your pain signals effectively.

Quite in all likelihood, the most difficult pain to cope with is long term pain that you could't control. This is typically because of a few form of scientific scenario like neuropathic pain or a herniated disc. When you've got a revel in of manage over the ache, you understand the pain as less extreme. Long-distance cyclists regularly enjoy their sport, but if someone had been pressured to motorbike for a hundred km, they'll in all likelihood discover it to be a completely unpleasant revel in.

When a few medical scenario motives your pain outdoor of your control, you may likely recognize the pain as extra extreme.

Additionally, some scientific conditions are likely to stay with you for years if not in your whole lifestyles. The excellent way to deal with this sort of ache is to use the identical technique which changed into stated earlier. Recognize the ache for what it's far, then outline it as a impartial revel in

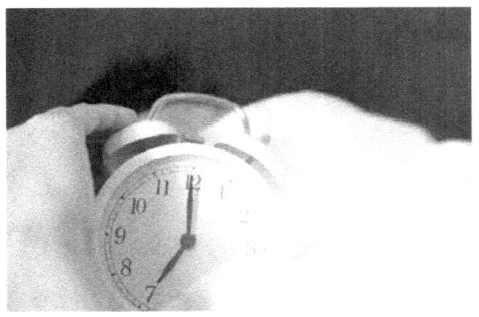

Chapter 8: Techniques To Beat Procrastination

Procrastination is determined in every element of our lives; it's the "infection" that isn't simply curable; it's most effective doable and taken underneath control. Procrastination technique to cast off, to get rid of, to remove, to find out excuses no longer to do, to discover some exclusive distraction, and so forth. People in any respect ranges cope with it – college students, youngsters, parents, experts, entrepreneurs, leaders, presidents… the excellent difference is that a few human beings are aware of it, those can fight it, and a few aren't aware of it, those don't fight it and are passive to it.

Types of Procrastination

Here are 8 styles of procrastination with examples of starting walking three times a week:

1) Thinking that it wishes to be best

Overthinking how jogging should be ideal interest is searching for outstanding routes that aren't too hard, no longer too easy with out an entire lot dust, without traffic, and plenty of others. Then, attempting to shop for perfect footwear – now not too ugly, no longer too quite, the ones that have thick sole... oh, and the shorts need to be perfectly becoming your thighs with zippered pockets, so you don't lose your mp3 participant. And the music... yeah, the song desires to be clearly interesting, so it motivates you, and you spend weeks in making an first-rate playlist so that you can preserve you going. Any of these sounds acquainted?

2) Not feeling like doing it (laziness)

Pure antique-university laziness is the most common and most recognizable. Feeling that you truely need to upward push up from your couch and exchange your garments to begin taking walks is certainly an excessive amount of. All that education and finding the route, then stretching in a while… You'll truely do it every different day, however no longer in recent times, you don't revel in find it irresistible proper now and also you need to experience it's the proper 2nd a good way to run.

3) Thinking you need to discover ways to do it first

Assuming which you want to study dozens of books in advance than you begin it and that you want to discover a educate who will teach you the manner to run. Because you aren't a professional runner, how can you sincerely go out and run? It's easy to do it incorrect and fail. You don't recognise what the proper tempo is for you, what elevation, what distance and how many heartbeats is too much… No, you need to have a train for this. Now it's even too complicated to look at it from a e-book.

four) Feeling intimidated of others and feeling afraid of failure

Comparing your self to extraordinary human beings that run six instances according to week, run 10 miles and you could only run, like, 1/2 of the mile. If you go out and run, you could face a herbal failure because of the fact you want to be a professional to start walking. Also, all unique runners are healthy and also you're now not. If you run now, it's a recipe for failure. Well, wager what? You run to get fit, no longer the alternative manner spherical!

five) Feeling fearful of your achievement

Feeling that you may do too properly at it and that in the end, all routes might be too clean for you, you'll outrun every of your peers or that you can lose too much weight and as a stop result, look to skinny and all garments will appear like it's setting on you. Believe me, I doubt that every body is that lucky that success comes that smooth in any element of lifestyles. On the other hand, in case you do grow to be a success in strolling that fast, it's the sweetest challenge you may face. So, prevent stressful, start running and you can see that the whole lot takes plenty of dedication, or your cause is certainly now not large enough. If that's the case, adapt your desires.

6) Worrying what other human beings assume/low conceitedness

Worrying about what will your friends, circle of relatives and friends say. Will they giggle at you? Will they receive as true with that is "out of your league"? These sorts of questions moreover display your low conceitedness. And an excessive amount of thinking about what fantastic people count on gained't get you anywhere. One element is for sure; humans will typically have their opinion on everything. Don't care what specific humans expect, really do what it feels right for you and start doing it.

7) Listening to super humans

There will in no manner be loss of humans's opinions, so taking note of distinctive people telling you that walking isn't that appropriate for your knees and ankles, that on foot takes too much time, that you ought to take the magic pill, and so on. Will in no manner get you everywhere. And don't forget me, a person will constantly offer you with horrible recommendation, it doesn't recall in case you even asked them for one. Listening to those recommendation received't get you everywhere similarly than they are. So, the least you could do is qualify who the person who gives you the recommendation is – if she or he has already accomplished what you would really like to do, then test from their revel in and stay committed in your purpose. But, if that individual is a ways faraway from your ideal position model – it's better to go away the room because of the fact they'll kill your dream with their bad mindset. Anyway, it's better to do what you supposed and discover a manner to acquire achievement, regardless of all of the recommendation. Committing to at least one concept through the years receives you on your cause.

Which leads us to...

eight) Not being committed to 1 desire

Does it sound familiar even as you get an concept of doing something, however whilst you start to analyze a hint bit, you find out that it takes a number of artwork?

It begins offevolved to scare you; you begin to take note of one-of-a-kind people's pieces of recommendation and/otherwise you start procrastinating the use of all 8 of those procrastination examples. As a result, you begin "leaping" from one factor to every other and no longer one of the mind are "precise enough" for committing to it. This is the case of a lack of vision and clarity. Refocus, rewrite your plan and decide to 1 problem over time till you grasp it. Running 3

instances each week is similar, due to the truth the consequences acquired't show for months. Sometimes even more if you don't encompass higher nutrients and additional exercise as time passes. Being committed and, as you get higher, consisting of more traumatic situations on your workout, will result in the success you want.

Chapter 9: Tips To Boost Your Motivation And Self Control

Grow Your Knowledge

The initial step to cultivating your self-self belief is making sure that you bought know-how both in your private and expert undertakings. There is continuously that vicinity for that you are feeling you lack in understanding and statistics.

If you need more self-self assurance, then you definately need to show mastery on this issue. You can increase your expertise via taking online courses, participating in comparable meetings and sports, on the thing of reading books. The distinct component that you could pleasure in at the same time as acquiring knowledge are teleclasses, in that you get to speak and participate in discussions collectively along with your friends. This goes to head a protracted way in enhancing your degree of self-self perception.

Appreciate Smaller Wins

Unshakeable self-self assurance originates from the capability to enjoy and have an excellent time little successes and victories. Consider this as presenting prizes for the usage of information. Do you endure in thoughts the element about micro-dreams? Well, whenever you advantage a micro-motive, you praise your self. Yes, they may be no longer the ideally suited goal, but they're little pieces that include the larger purpose.

The prize does now not need to be huge. Even a easy pat on the yet again or exceptional a honest praise from an accomplice is enough to enhance your level of self-self belief. For that cause, ensure that you display every little accomplishment and allow your self to enjoy it certainly. By doing this, you may begin to experience your self-self guarantee developing each single day.

Believe in Something

Among the developments I respect about assured people is they agree with in a exquisite being. They suppose that the maker of the universe has a function for each residing soul. Simply placed, the cause why we are on this planet right now could be to find and fulfill our more huge motive.

They seem to have first-rate statistics that after they agree to the plan of the writer, achieving success is sincerely a matter of time. For that reason, in case you absolutely desire to perform success, you want to trust that it is plausible. You have to have undeviating self belief for your capability. When your religion is loaded with enthusiasm, then there may be a immoderate chance that you're going to comply along with your real cause.

Cultivate A Firm Resolve

Within this lifestyles, it is herbal that you are going to address obstacles and frustrations inside the way. It is, because of this, herbal to experience mad and dissuaded. Nevertheless, you should see those troubles as a threat for analyzing for some element larger but to take place on your future.

When you show faith in your skills, you are going to surpass discouragements and get a strong solve. It is that this clear up this is going to, therefore, help you conquer annoying conditions. This is normally considering the reality that company solve is a actual mark of perseverance at paintings. Instead of despairing, you will recognize that without those issues, you may now not have a boom mind-set. Your mind want to be targeted on the popular give up result and not on obstructions. Rather than considering 1000 motives why you cannot, do not forget one cause why you can.

With time, you'll see your talents change into talents. It is in truth then that you're going to start to see what is surely possible, a diploma of achievement guiding you ahead with masses of energy and passion. It is that this passion that is going to preserve you ignited to hold scoring the ones little micro-goals.

Work With Professionals

Determine locations in which you have got were given gaps in information that you need to pinnacle off. As quickly as you try this, get help from experts which can be going that will help you in acquiring more information and experience. Understanding which you have experts' useful resource, you may be more assured even as performing and figuring out moreover. You can take a look at from specialists from books, blog internet websites, movies, cellphone calls, one-on-one meetings, workshops, and so forth. The advantage of an professional teach is that they may be going to assist you to live liable for each motion you are taking in finishing your utility.

Keep in mind that, if you choice self-self belief, you then actually need to attract in self-self belief. Yes, specialists are going to show you the manner. However, they'll be not going to stroll the road for you. You want to need to undergo all worrying conditions alongside side your head held excessive your eyes on the reward. Ultimately, you can arrive there.

Visualize Your Confident Self

When you could view yourself as any character confident, then self-self belief is going to come to be being a feature that is easy and natural to illustrate in reality. You start to revel in it straight away. Take a minute to test your self having the self-self assurance that you require in a particular scenario.

Picture how you may assume and behave if you had the self-self guarantee you are after. Preferably, near your eyes and be conscious your self utilising your thoughts's eye, performing with quite some self-self guarantee and conviction. Keep that picture to your thoughts, and you will apprehend that your vision goes to start taking root and coming real.

Believe That You Deserve Confidence

Did you understand that expectations are faith at work? At this 2nd, you have were given got presently imagined your self being self-assured and the way you could feel after that. When you are self-confident, you are going to talk, act, and circulate truely and with masses of ardour as you pursue your goals. This is while you understand which you have the sight, feelings, and actions of a self-confident character. Simply placed, you may be a long manner better positioned to perform hundreds extra than you predicted. When you count on to be confident, it includes fruition.

Like we've presently stated, self-self notion is not a few element that happens overnight. You want to place these actionable suggestions into exercise over months. Begin through jotting down methods in which you plan to use these movements. In this way, you recognize precisely how it would be like to behave within the course of your goal. When you act upon them, you start understanding vast improvements in your self-self notion, and short this equates to arrogance, pleasure, happiness, and high-quality fulfillment in lifestyles.

Chapter 10: Self-Discipline Habits

We have all visible how a lack of strength of mind can be one of the greatest obstacles to success. Increasing your electricity of will can move an extended manner in enhancing your possibility of achievement, and you could do this with the useful aid of fostering the following behavior:

Work on a few component which you are enthusiastic about

If you do a little issue that you are obsessed with, electricity of will will come truely. Self-vicinity, as we've seen, calls a good way to awareness in your middle obligations and maintain your self from doing what feels comfortable within the meanwhile. If you're pursuing a few factor for that you lack the ardour, it'll grow to be an uphill conflict. However, if you select out a few difficulty you revel in doing, it turns into notably a great deal much less

93

tough so that you can keep away from do and moreover to avoid procrastination.

Get rid of potential distractions

Self-disciplined humans have a propensity to do away with capability distractions in their environment. Self-field is set keeping off the topics that could thieve your focus a long way from the center topics that you want to paintings on. Instead of putting yourself in a role in that you need to fight distractions constantly, you could eliminate them inside the first location. For instance, if you have to art work on a assignment or to have a take a look at for the subsequent 6 hours, you could flip off all your emails, messages, and social media notifications. You might also additionally even turn off the internet in case you don't need it for paintings.

Do the maximum hard matters first

In many instances, we will be inclined to get caught at the same time as running on projects due to the truth the responsibilities we are doing have variable tiers of issue. If you have got were given were given been doing easy duties for some time, then come upon one hard task, your possibilities of stopping or losing interest can boom significantly. In order to live disciplined, start via the usage of doing the toughest thing/s or those who'll take the longest to complete, first. Go over your complete task and determine out which individual duties are the maximum concerned, then schedule your workflow in the type of way that the ones obligations get finished first. Once you are carried out with the tough matters, it's downhill from there.

Make speedy selections

Indecisiveness is one of the primary motives why human beings are not capable of reputation on their paintings and live self-disciplined. Sometimes, we waste time gathering "greater facts" in preference to performing. To make fast picks, you want to workout consultation of a conviction that "completed is higher than first-class." It's better to finish a few aspect it's far you want to do, in location of wasting time searching for to determine out the way to do it flawlessly. That's due to the truth perfection is a fallacy, and too much facts results in "analysis paralysis."

The following bodily video games will assist you to study powerful electricity of thoughts conduct:

Forcing yourself to get started out

In this exercising, we're going that will help you do some thing you have been fending off for a while. Find some thing which you have imagined to do. It can be a ebook that you desired to examine, a damaged object in your own home that you have intended to repair or a home-improvement task that you have imagined to cope with. The chances are that you have created a motive in your mind to rationalize your state of no hobby. Maybe you're telling your self which you want extra information, more time, more money, and masses of others.

Now, ask yourself, "What's the first step I want to take to get this finished?" Force your self to take that step. It doesn't depend in case you are prepared or not; just get began.

You will realize that starting is the difficult issue, and that while you get the ball rolling, and you stay on route, the undertaking can be finished in no time.

Make your bed

Making your bed simplest takes a couple of minutes. However, lots of us don't do it.

Why? Because there may be no reason to do it, and no effect if we fail to do it. Making your bed is an act of area, and it could cross an extended manner in supporting you live a extra primarily based life. As the announcing is going, the devil is within the information.

Tomorrow morning while you upward thrust up, the number one element you want to do is go through the motions of nicely making your bed. In those 2 mins as quickly as you have got up, you may excessive yourself to be in a efficient nation, and you'll be surprised at how masses more disciplined you'll be in some unspecified time inside the future of the relaxation of the day.

Chapter 11: Practicing Self Discipline

An ounce of self –area is sufficient to make the whole lot viable, but without it, even the maximum common and best intention can appear not viable to acquire. Self-situation is described as having the ability to govern your mind and feelings, which results in controlling behavior and characteristic yourself take movement in a specific way.

Usually, this relates to a outstanding exchange or some problem that veers you a long way from a negative direction. It is closely related to having energy of mind, this is the capability to delay gratification. This method that to acquire prolonged-term desires, one want that allows you to resist quick-time period temptations. It additionally means we should be capable of manage our feelings and that during spite of horrible feelings, one is able to hire a cool head in the face of difficult conditions. Thus, strength of will is a aware law of yourself that requires attempt and strength of mind.

Because we are humans, there are various instances wherein we discover ourselves to be lacking in power of thoughts or power of mind. For instance, you recognize you could want to awaken early tomorrow for artwork, however you find your self although looking tv way past middle of the night. Or, at the same time as you solve to get right right into a fitness utility, you can't sit up straight for cheat day and simply "have a piece" of a meals that's now not part of your diet plan. Or, at the same time as you're told by using manner of the use of your medical doctor to prevent smoking, however the sight or smell of a cigarette makes you provide in (and provide you with an excuse), consequently making you fall again into the dependancy.

There are such a number of extra examples, and I'm sure all people have been there. But while we determine to do addiction stacking to efficiently include a fine addiction, we want a whole lot of electricity of mind and electricity of will. It is what gadgets one guy other than all others, lifts him up from mediocrity and despite others having the abilties or assets to do the same reason, people with strength of will and electricity of will will normally discover themselves a fulfillment in achieving the topics they need.

The first element you want to do is to set up the motivation for alternate. It should be compelling sufficient. Let's say you are heading off similarly scientific complications, so that you determine to prevent smoking. Or, probably it's far some factor you're enthusiastic about, like a life-prolonged dream to compete professionally in swimming. Whatever the inducement is, it wishes to be strong and compelling sufficient to maintain the ball rolling.

Next, you need to show screen your behavior towards that purpose. You need to need it so badly that you may exhaust all technique to collect your cause.

The final problem is the electricity of thoughts. It is the unmarried most important detail that allows you get subjects finished and get you towards your desired very last consequences. Your capacity to set yourself easy goals and work in the route of them every unmarried day will already guarantee your achievement, and no great issue comes even close to sheer electricity of mind. Just as a durable building calls for an awesome basis, a extraordinary amount of strength of will should start early on, even earlier than making a decision to work to your dreams.

When you need to aim for drastic changes to your existence, recognize that failure regularly tags alongside. Being too bold allows you flow into quicker and further competitive, however this will purpose fake preference syndrome. False choice syndrome is whilst you set unrealistic expectancies approximately yourself and your desires. While it's first-rate to be high-quality, it's better to be practical. For example, you propose to prevent smoking in each week surely, however you currently smoke two packs of cigarettes consistent with day. While the purpose is admirable, it truly honestly isn't practical for optimum humans.

False choice syndrome makes it hard for the individual that embarks on a addiction-stacking journey to attain goals with the modern-day property or timelines he has to be had. People have a propensity to anticipate very in particular approximately their desires. They need to gather higher and large subjects in faster techniques. While there may be no longer anything terrible approximately questioning huge, the whole photograph needs to be taken into consideration. When one is unmindful of the time and sources it takes to accumulate a goal, it presents the right recipe for a fast burnout.

This will in the end motive quitting. It then turns into a vicious cycle, one which makes human beings continuously fall sufferer to the syndrome of making common attempts to trade themselves however fail to accomplish that. Instead of going all out, PLAN your success in small steps, as a machine, with a non-prevent wave of little movements in case you want to stack up and reason greater awesome consequences.

Willpower takes some of electricity, and on the same time as you're confused, it eats up everything – a while, your stress, your interest, and your ardour for preserving shifting beforehand. You might likely have located that within the maximum traumatic instances to your lifestyles, you generally have a tendency to take delight in volatile and terrible behavior – overeating or no longer consuming enough, smoking, eating or doing each unique satisfies of different types to experience exquisite. These movements may be very, very tough to manipulate and get away of.

By doing these things, we enjoy a temporary feeling of satisfaction that takes us some distance from the topics that pressure us. However, the ones strain responses take in a lot of your willpower. Stress impairs the emotional manipulate of someone, consequently making it tough for one to perform the deliberate obligations. Therefore, that permits you to workout electricity of will efficaciously, you want to work on reducing your stress levels.

One of the precept motives why human beings revel in a loss of power of mind is that we commonly have a tendency to allocate more time to sports than they need to get it finished. Because of this, there can be the temptation to set aside the work for later, primary to stress to finish the entirety.

To counter, allocate lesser time for any specific interest, whether or not it's urgent or no longer, and this may substantially lessen the opportunity of you drifting some distance from the art work that desires to be completed. Now which you are made privy to why strength of mind has tendencies to fail, you need to now have a more unique draw close of the belongings you have to and have to now not do to hold on in your strength of mind.

The environment you are in moreover plays a massive element for your self-control competencies. Let's say you want to shed pounds, but your kitchen is complete of chocolates and different risky food due to the truth the people you stay with regularly snack on these things. In the form of situation, it'll be complex on the way to lose the weight you would really like to. It will take strength of mind and power of will, however those gadgets furthermore depleted in the long run. The strength you can have used for workout may be spent in controlling and resisting your temptations, main to electricity of will fatigue.

You want to be in an surroundings that allows the behavior or behavior you need to increase. Similarly, social have an effect on and social community systems play a totally high-quality function in modeling behaviors. Does this endorse you need to abandon your circle of relatives or buddies that don't useful resource the environment you need to alternate? Of direction no longer! What you could do is restriction your affiliation with humans or special influences because it pertains to the ones sports.

For instance, you need to increase a addiction of waking up early, but your companion enjoys searching TV till late at night on a bed room television. You can suggest that the TV be moved outdoor the mattress room or decide to sleep in every other bedroom. In this way, the affiliation is probably lessen off, and you may successfully examine thru together together with your plan. To similarly your dependancy-stacking sports activities, are seeking out out nearby places wherein like-minded humans hold out and be a part of that institution.

When we talk approximately self-discipline, there may be constantly the danger of temptations. Removing or staying faraway from those distractions in your surrounding environment is an critical first step while running in the course of strength of will. The most dangerous factor is to assume you have got an infinite deliver and reservoir of self-control, so in preference to spending electricity on trivial everyday topics, keep this for the use of your energy of mind for immoderate-cost selections. Also, once more, make adjustments to create a supportive surroundings and you'll be amazed to look the modifications that come on the issue of it.

To in addition enhance your power of mind and self-discipline, proper right here are other sports activities you could do: Mindfulness

Mindfulness is not some factor this is truely restrained to the religious journey undertaken with the aid of the use of Buddhist clergymen. Mindfulness is the eye that arises thru the simple act of paying hobby on motive, being in the 2nd, and being located in a non-judgmental manner. It is a manner of traveling inner your thoughts and body to decorate recognition spherical you, about your mind and feelings inner your self.

Activities for mindfulness encompass body experiment, conscious yoga, and sitting meditation. These sports can be finished every day for at least thirty to 40 minutes. When one gets higher at meditating, it allows boom a giant sort of self-discipline abilities together with consciousness, hobby, impulse manage, pressure control, self-attention, and hobby. Meditation can with out problem be executed with the aid of the use of sitting silently collectively along with your spine right away and being focused for your breath.

Quality sleep

If you continuously deprive your body of getting enough rest and sleep at night time time time, you are already within the throes of developing anxiety and pressure. Sleep deprivation impacts your temper, cognitive overall performance, and motor feature. It additionally impacts your working reminiscence, better cognitive functions and government hobby. Lack of sleep ends in emotions of exhaustion really due to the fact your cells may additionally additionally have trouble soaking up the glucose they need from the precept bloodstream in case you are worn-out. In such conditions, the body wants to preserve what little energy is left with the intention to protect your mind in case of an emergency.

Get up and begin moving

Physical exercise has numerous advantages for your frame at such an much less luxurious cost. Moving spherical has the potential to enhance your strength of will to a huge amount. Your body can get in form on the equal time as your mental electricity improves. It moreover permits relieve strain, dangerous cravings, and is a powerful anti-depressant.

Chapter 12 (The Short One)

Something You Must Know First

"Where there's difficulty, there may be order and right fortune."

Niccolo Machiavelli (1469 -1527)

WITH THIS BOOK you´ll get all the electricity of thoughts you need. You´ll collect any purpose.

But be realistic.

Be sensible due to the truth in the course of the method you´ll undergo relapses. Quitting smoking, doing away with junk food, or handling it gradual higher can have its usaand downs.

And there you may need to keep going.

But do not worry. First because of the reality proper here you´ll discover all of the techniques to emerge as self-disciplined all of the time. You´ll get over any relapse. Where every person quits, you could keep going.

Accept also that it'll be threatening to many which you try and exchange. It will scare them to lack of existence. There can be envy. They might not together with you turning into better, and consequently turning into higher than them. Count on it. Count on it however actually have a study your way. Because gambling to be just like the majority isn't for you.

You'll become unstoppable that manner.

But pay interest, with splendid power comes tremendous duty. Make proper use of the gadget you'll discover. They will will can help you bypass a long way. But moreover assist others alongside aspect your new electricity.

Chapter 13: How To Eliminate Indiscipline Knowing Its Three Roots

"Every failure teaches a person a few factor, if he's going to but take a look at."

Charles Dickens (1812-1871), British author

A SURE WAY TO GET disciplined is coming across in which your indiscipline comes from. If you understand your enemy you obtained´t lose.

Quitting procrastination or overeating may be smooth whilst you see the cause. Find the inspiration and you've got the answer. And moreover lessen destiny rebellions of indiscipline. Because you aren´t condemned to replicate your past.

Why you've got become undisciplined

Your indiscipline isn't always inherited. Nobody turn out to be born procrastinating, longing for eating fast-meals, or losing time on infinite coffee breaks. Indiscipline is a sum of repeated behaviors that these days appearance natural.

And like everything you located out at the identical time as developing up, your indiscipline changed into moreover built thru gazing others. Perhaps you discovered that escaping from artwork changed into what clever humans did. Only losers worked, even as the good ones succeeded with smart arguments. Or you noticed that spending cash decreased disappointment. Or that TV modified into crucial to lighten up. And those fake assumptions produced lousy behavior.

And now you believe you studied that those behavior are a part of you. A kind of fashionable aspect of you, "Indiscipline is a part of my character!" But no, this isn´t you. You are an entire lot better. You aren´t condemned to duplicate your beyond. Your lifestyles need to not be a chain of u.S.And downs in which you simplest extinguish fires and never advantage your desires.

So first forget about about beyond errors. "Not many do nicely from the begin," as Roman philosopher Seneca said. And then analyze the 3 vital motives of your indiscipline. You´ll kill any indiscipline decrease back-engineering to the on the spot wherein it appeared like a awesome drift. Know your enemy you´ll beat him.

Cause 1: The well-known guy from college

Do you undergo in mind at the same time as the well-known boy from school started to smoke? "Me too," stated the enthusiasts of the cool guy. They knew it damage their health, how many human beings preferred their first cigarette? But they usual the damage to enter the aristocracy of folks who smoke. Quitting smoking? No thank you. I´m too cool.

And then nicotine made the relaxation. To enjoy well they wished a cigarette. And they fooled themselves through pronouncing "One day I´ll give up." Later additionally that they had a chum with emphysema. But their addiction emerge as stronger.

Kids are too vulnerable and appreciate often the wrong man or woman. And if the famous guy procrastinates, lies, or smokes, they´ll duplicate his indiscipline.

SOLUTION:

Follow your way. The well-known guy with a awful dependancy isn't cool. He´s stupid.

Cause 2: The false belief

A little obese woman have become tortured through her schoolmates being referred to as fatty. Today she eats compulsively to preserve being fat.

Another boy escaped from an unfair punishment way to a lie. So he repeated that approach. Today he is a compulsive liar.

Another worried boy have turn out to be knowledgeable thru his trainer in front of his classmates, "Don´t assume masses!" And all people laughed. Today he survives running in low-paid jobs.

False beliefs and absence of state of affairs go hand in hand. The international is whole of people with appropriate intentions however a distorted imaginative and prescient condemned them. A awful statement, a incorrect feature version, or a misinform stay to inform the story, and they were given caught right right right into a entice.

Those humans bounce today from task to technique without progressing. They recall they won´t win a few element through giving the pleasant of themselves. They blame others for being caught and take delivery of as real with that society owes them more time to loosen up. And to treatment stress there are fantastic drugs.

SOLUTION:

Revise what they cautioned you because of the fact it can be false. Take a awful addiction and ask: "What did I pay attention as quickly as approximately this addiction?" Find the foundation and root it out.

Cause 3: The unstable consolation

Relaxing relieved you from that excessive paintings. Procrastinating that massive venture moreover relieved you. A large meal after a demanding situation furthermore relieved you... But now you maintain enjoyable, procrastinating, and consuming greater to feel nicely. It seems like it modified into in your terrific hobby.

And at the same time, a powerful advertising and marketing enterprise makes billions growing products to relieve you: Take a break... Eat that sweet... You deserve it...

But reliefs kill your possibilities. And worse, they have a propensity to expand. A coffee manner two extra cookies... A beer manner a cigarette... An greater day of tour implies consuming more... Comfortable but risky reliefs.

SOLUTION:

Revise your reliefs and made them steadily shorter. Insist one minute more with that undertaking. Resist 1/2 of an ice cream. In small steps it won´t price you.

¿Which of the above instances is yours? Once you recognize the basis, getting rid of indiscipline may be plenty much less complicated. You aren´t condemned to replicate beyond errors.

Chapter 2 - KEYS

-1-

Your indiscipline isn't always inherited. No one changed into born with a bent to procrastinate, overeat, or waste time.

-2-

Kill the basis of indiscipline and you´ll kill indiscipline.

-3-

The root of your indiscipline can be clearly a wrong remark or a feature model with lousy conduct. Find it and you´ll change speedy.

Chapter 14: Goals: The Key Of Self-Discipline

"The issue of writing a few problem down is step one towards making it take vicinity."

Lee Iacocca (1924-2019), Visionary automaker

I´M SURE YOU´VE HEARD about the strength of designing your desires. But at the same time, it is easy postponing it for a few special day.

Yet in case you format your desires proper, you gained´t most effective revolutionize your existence and get outcomes speedy, you can robotically advantage all of the strength of will you want.

So first be very smooth about what you want to attain in life. And the vital component therefore is not proscribing your big dream. Because to create something huge, first you want a outstanding picture for your mind. The first region tour have become an image within the thoughts of an engineer. And La Gioconda, the Empire State Building, or any mythical music modified into additionally first an photograph within the mind of someone we now name genius.

And the identical goes on your life. You´ll advantage all of the energy of thoughts you need in case you first layout your huge goals. And therefore comply with those steps:

STEP 1: How To Design Your Goals Smartly

STEP 2: Plan And Break It Down To Get Self-Disciplined

First is the what, 2nd the how. Or like Henry David Thoreau said: "Build castles in the air... And then positioned the pointers underneath them."

STEP 1:

HOW TO DESIGN YOUR GOALS SMARTLY

Those who succeeded with strength of mind identified that it have become easy desires what gave them electricity.

But the manner most humans format their goals is incorrect. Most see it as writing a listing. Yet you need to do it proper.

First, you have to assume huge. Really large. Then you need to subdivide it into smaller chunks and plan the ones movements. Later I'll display you the way. But first factor excessive. You can climb Mount Everest, construct a multinational, or gain a few thing you want. Yet first you want specific numbers. For instance, if you need to be wealthy, how masses cash do you want to have? And on the same time as? Or if you want to be a extremely good mountaineer, how can you climb the fourteen 8.000. And the cash to do it?

Numbers and closing dates are critical. It's a fun exercise too. Not only will you internalize it better, however you may also experience making plans it.

The question then is, why do no longer people plan their dreams?

Because they do now not recognize how important it's miles. They surely anticipate they don't have time to set desires, "I truely have too much to do!"

What???

Do you've got time to examine emails, take transport of interruptions, and watch TV, however cannot set aside time to format some factor as… your lifestyles?

If you do not have time to format your desires, you'll keep having no time. And you'll be unhappy. You'll fall into the vicious circle of persevering with in a interest you hate and so keep with out easy thoughts... To maintain being a slave of a venture you hate. Because without dreams, you´ll art work for the desires of others.

So harm the cycle. Be smarter than ninety 5% of people and make your goals the most essential element now. I assure that simply with the useful aid of thinking about them, you´ll see tactics to get self-disciplined and do the whole thing faster. Any minute you quite truly lie down thinking about your desires, may be your high-quality investment. Because right here comes the essential component: the hours you spend making plans will save you as a minimum 10 times the ones hours.

One hour designing dreams suggest 10 hours of extra artwork stored. Because you´ll see shortcuts and answers. And specifically, you´ll see that it´s viable. It acquired´t be a much dream anymore.

So the time has come. What have to you honestly like to gather in life? What career do you actually need? Where do you want to live? With whom?

Clarity!

Sit down till you be conscious it. It won't be sitting with out troubles, it is going to be the most critical hassle you may do, designing your existence.

Clarity!

Many wanted a painful revel in to transform their lives. An infection that almost killed them, a economic spoil, a worrying break out to a cutting-edge u . S .... But the ones excessive conditions helped them to discover their actual vocation. Yet why not find out it with out ache? You really have to take a seat down down evenly and format your dreams.

So prevent dropping time with urgencies and brief-time period duties, and set apart time to expect.

Clarity!

Do why some humans succeed over humans with extra skills? Because they without a doubt have easy desires. This makes them hundreds more focused and compensates their loss of information. People who went some distance planned their desires. Clarity became their motto.

Life is brief, do not waste it. Lack of goals and diffuse thoughts are an explosive cocktail. Why art work hard plenty of hours if it's miles now not aligned collectively with your desires? That's why all the time you spend designing your goals may be your top notch funding.

So ask your self… Where do you want to transport? What is your extraordinary passion?

And do not make the error of giving the respectable solution. "I need more money and a nice house through the ocean. Oh... And specific fitness."

Too unmeasurable.

Don´t be naïve. Without numbers and last dates, you gained´t waft anywhere. And you received´t align your life together along with your goals. Because you can not pursue a million bucks whilst looking for a regular mission as a public reliable. (You'd be surprised what number of humans count on so). You gained´t additionally collect your private organization if on the same time you have buddies that only keep in mind claiming rights and escaping from work. You´ll outperform nice when you have a reason and pursue it.

So recognize that first you have to save you appearing. First you must suppose and locate your actual dream. Only with clean dreams you´ll come to be disciplined. Only then you definately definately definitely´ll save you wasting years on secondary responsibilities. Those who went a long way had readability of cause. Steven Spielberg knew thinking about a infant that he loved filmmaking. And Charlie Chaplin desperately desired to be an actor. And your favored entrepreneur moreover knew precisely what he preferred.

So stop and ask yourself, are you strolling tough with out consequences? Revisit your goals in that case. I suggest in fact prevent and assume. Review beyond mistakes and format new desires. You´ll see how the whole thing adjustments from that second. And consequently stop and sit down frivolously. Everybody believes they already anticipate even as doing different matters. But they quality get lost in short-time period thoughts that don't have anything to do with their actual dreams. And so they spend their complete life. Going nowhere.

But you´ll only flow some distance in case you set dreams. Because only so you´ll see that a good buy of what you do doesn´t serve you. It might be a marvel, but moreover accurate information. Because you´ll see you've got got time for what´s absolutely vital. Now you think you're caught in a mountain of pending obligations, however suppose in solitude and also you´ll see that not whatever is what it appears. And that you can collect your huge dream if you reorder your priorities.

Be cautious, in spite of the truth that, because many people will try to persuade you pronouncing they'll be "not ambitious," on the same time as giving the word ambition a awful connotation. But they lie. We all have pursuits. Yet maximum are too lazy to plot their movements and conceal it as a lack of ambition. But it´s even though laziness. The mother of all vices.

That's why you want to shake your mind and make clear your dreams. Does your paintings fulfill you? Do you want your life-style? Or located in reality: are you working to your massive dream?

Many do no longer dare to consider their goals because it implies looking into the black hole of a lifestyles they don´t want. And to run away they maintain themselves busy with meaningless obligations. But in case you want to go a long way you ought to damage that cycle.

First the reality.

Only at the identical time as you decide to layout your actual dream an excellent global will open. Will your to-do list increase? Maybe. But you may additionally gather it faster. Because right making plans will make you very disciplined. With clean desires, correct conduct will emerge. You´ll automatically be extra powerful and get effects. And higher, in case you plan nicely you may see the way to do the entirety in an lousy lot tons less time. Because every hour you intend you store 10 greater hours.

6 Questions to design the destiny you need

If you are now in that phase wherein you come what may additionally realize your massive reason, but it hasn't pretty crystallized, assist yourself with the following 6 questions. You do not need the right solution. All the time you recall it is going to be gold.

Ask your self:

1. What's the undertaking for that you could not wait to leap some distance from mattress within the morning?

2. In what talents are you higher than others?

three. Would you hold in your cutting-edge-day undertaking for the rest of your lifestyles?

four. Would you maintain collectively with your contemporary social circle forever?

5. What's your bottleneck to undertaking your goals?

6. How must you switch your passion proper right into a commercial company?

These questions may be hard at the start. Looking again and seeing the time you wasted isn't great. But you must cross that wall. Only so that you'll align paintings with what you love to do. Only so answers will come. And therefore ask yourself… Am I within the right vicinity? Am I living my dream? Am I operating on my energy?

You could make clear this with a friend (only with a person you preserve in mind). You´ll be amazed at his or her response. We are very subjective at the same time as studying ourselves, but very correct to peer the fact in others.

So first understand in that you are and in which you want to move. What are your dreams? And which obligations carry you within the direction of them? Simply examine. You´ll discover the way you exceptional artwork a small part of some time on something that gives you 80% of profits. And so that you´ll expand it. Enough of unimportant telephone calls, meaningless paperwork, and plenty extra meaningless meetings. Now you´ll take the bull with the resource of the horns. Your dreams first. And on paper.

Do you regret awful past movements? If you layout your desires after which write them, this received't take location. You´ll odor extremely good opportunities. Because you´ll have a radar to come across them. Hundreds of limitations will appear, however along with your huge intention on paper, you´ll locate continuously a solution. The secret is continually having your big dream present. If essential, write it moreover on a Post-It you put on your PC show display.

If you don't format your goals your pending duties will expand till occupying a hundred% of it slow. It´s certainly without a doubt one in every of Murphy's laws. Yet with easy dreams, the whole thing will make a contribution to them. So layout your targets thoroughly first. And then write them. This will recommend transforming your to-do list. This will mean making numbers and recalculating deadlines. And especially, this may propose constantly thinking about your desires. As a eternal guide. But so that you´ll get all your selections proper.

After having your desires designed is probably no matter the reality that grey days? Yes. But now it's miles going to be remarkable. Your new mistakes will boost up the entirety due to the fact they´ll assist you to know in which to transport. New duties will arise, however you´ll finish an awful lot quicker. If you take the bull through the horns designing and writing your dreams, the whole thing will help you. Even the limits. Especially the limitations. Nothing to do with how a tremendous deal you procrastinate now. You´ll input the elite of the exquisite-effective ones.

So to format your desires proper, follow this three-step method. From right here you´ll advantage all of the energy of will you want.

The 3 keys to format your goals

You can't waste your existence with art work that does not encourage you. This is also the vital component to getting disciplined.

But consequently first make easy and layout your goals precisely. Will it mean the rollercoaster of reading your modern-day-day existence? Yes. Will you need to redecorate many stuff you do? Yes. The ones who succeeded confronted their ghosts first. They first identified what they definitely wanted however did now not dare. It modified into hard to appearance the time they misplaced. Yet it became their fantastic pass. Because truely so that they sooner or later jumped.

So proper right here are the three keys to designing your desires and accomplishing them:

KEY 1:

WRITE DOWN EVERYTHING YOU WANT TO ACHIEVE. EVERYTHING!

No limits. As in case you could not fail.

KEY 2:

DESCRIBE YOUR IDEAL LIFE

Now the info. If you awaken each morning with $10 million to your account, how could your day be? Don't do not forget your self on a Caribbean seashore. The day is actually too lengthy. You need some aspect more to inspire you.

KEY three:

DECIDE: WHAT WOULD YOU DO IF YOU ONLY HAD ONE YEAR TO LIVE?

This will installation your priorities.

And now permit's use it on your case:

1. WRITE DOWN EVERYTHING YOU WOULD LIKE TO ACHIEVE. EVERYTHING!

First you need to suppose large. What can also need to you want to advantage in case you couldn't fail? Would you live on your preferred metropolis or ought to you select a house inside the country? Would you continue to upward thrust up early inside the morning to growth your corporation? Would you work while visiting the area for your sailboat? Would you retire one month each one year to Tibet to meditate? Would you be healthy in your 90´s?

Dare to dream.

And consequently be privy to your inner voice. It will guide you for your real purpose in case you listen. Every minute listening to your most profound voice is gold. So no limits. If you truly reason for additonal, you´ll benefit greater. As the Greeks stated, if you aim excessive whilst taking pictures an arrow, it'll generally go farther than if you motive for a medium distance. Failing and getting handiest 50% from 1,000 is infinitely higher than succeeding at getting 100% from 10. So purpose for a massive purpose first. It´s now not time to be timid.

And as quickly as you have got your wonderful intention positioned it on paper. This is fundamental. Write down all your desires and subgoals. Don't fear, you´ll continuously be able to regulate the records.

When you write your private and financial goals a present day electricity of will will push you. And coincidences you in no manner imagined will begin to arise.

And after writing them down, complete them with the two following steps.

2. DESCRIBE YOUR IDEAL LIFE

The tendency at the same time as designing your incredible life is to count on you´ll lie inside the solar at a luxury inn the complete day. But be given as actual with me, you acquired´t do it all the time. You´ll though have loads of time left. What will you do then? Seriously, what may additionally want to you do if you awoke within the morning with ten million dollars in your financial institution account?

Be realistic. With cash, hundreds of coins, there may be additionally u.S. Of americaand downs. You can´t birthday celebration every day. You'd become bored. You´ll also have to keep away from tempting food to live longer. You´ll additionally want to hold near your thoughts.

Be cautious because of the truth most humans´s solution is simply too naive; they're saying they would not mind being bored. But they don't know that boredom is more painful than being busy. And it additionally results in self-destruction. It's why human beings with cash come to be with tablets and damage their lives.

That's why it's so important designing your best day first. You ought to combine your new coins with a few thing to do and better contributors of the family. It's not sufficient to honestly disconnect. There are 24 hours consistent with day.

And when you format your new ideal life-style, the salt. Clear your priorities. Time is limited and you want to improvement fast.

three. DECÍDE: WHAT WOULD YOU DO IF YOU ONLY HAD ONE YEAR TO LIVE?

And now allow´s introduce the price issue. This is difficult however will boost up your dreams. Ask your self: what would you do if you quality had 3 hundred and sixty 5 days to live?

If although doubtful approximately your priorities, here´s wherein your actual you could seem. The mark you need to go away. Something you could regret all of your lifestyles if you hadn't attempted.

Introducing the 12-months time limit may be the final push to find your authentic passion. All in a unmarried, appearing much like the excellent and dwelling in the 2nd. And on the identical time spending time with folks that in truth remember. Crucial to field your self and benefit your dreams.

Thanks to those 3 steps you´ll be more efficient and characteristic extra time way to removing obligations that don´t healthful your big dream. The first advantage. The 2d one is that with clean desires you´ll get self-disciplined robotically.

Silvia's tale

I endure in thoughts Silvia, a latest graduate who did the preceding 3-step exercising to figure out her goals. When it changed into flip to goal excessive, she discovered out that her real dream turn out to be to live travelling the sector. Not the regular answer of human beings with new cash. It was honestly something she desired above everything else. Obviously this became not feasible, as a graduate she had no cash. But she further wrote her dream.

After that, what a twist of destiny, she had been given a interest in a tour company. And because the interest end up associated with visiting, her true ardour, she did it very well. And that allowed her to visit different nations to test motels and routes. And after continuing to paintings difficult, the employer gave her more trips. Yet on the identical time, as her massive reason modified into so severe, on the same time as seeing the sector she wrote adventure guides in her little free time. She first posted them on a weblog and then have turn out to be them into books. Her passion drove her to jot down down so enthusiastically that her guides have been in the long run a fulfillment. And nowadays, in spite of the reality that she have to retire with the royalties of her books, she but travels and keeps writing. It´s her ardour.

Do you moreover may additionally surprise the manner to make a living from your passion? The key is first clearing goals. Otherwise you´ll wander off in secondary obligations. You count on you do some detail however you pass nowhere.

Imagine for example you decide to decorate your tennis degree. It's a seductive intention. Beating all of your friends and being the incredible participant! But suppose yet again, do you really want to scouse borrow time from your big purpose to win a tennis suit? Are you going to allow your ego thieve your big dream? That's why you need to be very smooth approximately what you need. Is what you do associated with your big purpose? Really? Because best so that you´ll get rid of suicidal selections like losing three each day hours with tennis. Think approximately it, do you really want to expose off inside the the front of your pals? Maybe half of of-hour of every day running are sufficient to get in shape.

You ought to have crystal smooth goals. If tennis is your outstanding passion bypass for it. But allow it pass if it isn´t number one. Stay targeted. Your dream is extra crucial than the present day-day style.

So to any amount further do no longer waste any minute and format your actual dreams. Time is not a chewing gum you can stretch. Yet you´ll win electricity and in addition area on your mind in case you get rid of the needless.

And consequently recognize that maximum of your responsibilities are driven through the ego. So say no. Let bypass eighty% of your tasks and function one or at maximum massive desires. And the rest? Eliminate it.

And now you´ll ask your self... However how can I make a dwelling from my ardour?

The key to making money collectively together with your new strength of mind

Maybe you don´t pursue your dream for worry of losing your monthly paycheck. But you´ll earn an awful lot more if you observe your ardour. And faster than you keep in mind you studied. Yet therefore recognize this: your big intention want to remedy a trouble to others.

This is essential. You exceptional can win cash collectively along with your ardour if you provide a services or products that lets in a person.

Most humans fail with their dream because they lack one element: focusing their passion on assisting others. It's not enough to set up a website collectively with your hobby. It's no longer enough to excursion if that is what you need. Nor you cannot just examine astronomy books. You have to art work to your ardour in the sort of way that solves a want.

And therefore research first what the marketplace needs. And then as an instance excursion the sector on the equal time as publishing excursion publications, like Silvia. Or sell astronomy guides to beginners. There are many possibilities.

Passion and fixing a problem: this is the vital problem to dwelling from your first rate intention. And live very well. The Tournament Method to win power of thoughts

In the preceding three-step approach you observed the manner to format your huge motive. Yet possibly you continue to hesitate... Because you have got were given had been given more than one big purpose. Which is the actual one? Follow the Tournament Method to discover it out.

The Tournament Method

1. Write your goals on a listing

You now have numerous dreams and they all seem further vital. The wooden do not will let you see the wooded area. So first write them down. The order does not depend range.

2. Take contiguous goals and pick out the winner

Start with the number one desires of your list and decide this is greater crucial. The winner will pass to the following spherical. Like in a event. What reason is greater critical, incomes enough to shop for a Mercedes convertible or having greater hours a day on your family? Then go to the subsequent pair, what do you select out, 20 mins of yoga or developing your Twitter account? Choose the winners and pass them to the subsequent round.

After the number one spherical, simplest half of the desires will stay. Then undergo your listing once more and preserve evaluating goals. Each winner will over again bypass to the following round. (If you've got an impaired huge type of desires honestly have a look at three at a time). Continue the wholesome until playing the quarterfinals, semifinals, and the final. The winner will be manifestly your big goal.

There you've got it, the cause you´ll placed above the whole lot.

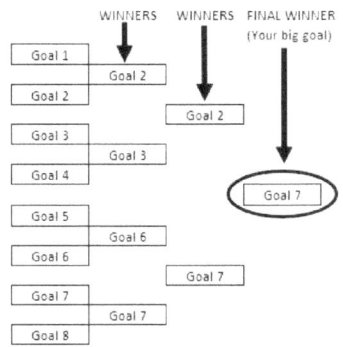

The fit technique to make easy your goals constantly works. You can use it additionally to find out your 2d maximum vital cause, the zero.33 one, etc. So you´ll moreover eliminate coronary coronary heart-breaking conflicts like choosing amongst career or own family existence. Because the lots debated preference about loose time or career, repeated ad nauseam in films and magazine articles, has no feel. The key is knowing what you want. Then no choice may be painful.

Success is going for humans with smooth dreams. And therefore you need to select out. You ought to make an effort to figure it out. Otherwise you could waste your life in a hobby you hate and pursue colourful gadgets that are scams.

Yet have clean dreams and you´ll reap belongings you even do not forget. On one hand, you´ll make appropriate choices and strength of will will appear robotically. And at the opportunity, you´ll live intensely every 2nd. Even a Monday morning may be a part of your wonderful journey.

Everything will come with out problems as quick as you understand what you want. "Give me a place to stand, and I shall go with the flow the world," because the Greek Archimedes said.

And now, when you designed your goals and wrote them down, take the second step, making plans proper to collect them rapid.

STEP 2:

 PLAN AND BREAK IT DOWN TO GET SELF-DISCIPLINED

By designing your desires, you took the maximum crucial step. Beginning and seeing it´s viable. And now allow´s see a manner to benefit them in file time: planning proper. First the what and now comes the how.

To cross a protracted manner you want to isolate time to plan. You should map out your quick-term and prolonged-time period movements. You want to reassign priorities. You want to recalculate your schedules. You have to plot. Because not planning is making plans to fail.

We communicate approximately manage structures, artwork-existence balance, personal mentors, and special fancy inclinations, however achievement is as clean as putting aside extra time to the antique school wondering. It's nonetheless the amazing element you could do to exchange your life. And of path, it will decorate your self-control.

Try it. Isolate your self for a few minutes each day considering what you may do better and you´ll without delay see techniques to win time. You´ll combine certain responsibilities with others to multiply your productiveness. You´ll even see there are various duties you do no longer even need to do. That the alternative desire is wasting months with extra art work.

The time you spend making plans will come up with 10 X more time!

Remember the alternative day when you needed to cross midway domestic to select out up a report you forgot?

If you had spent one minute, only one minute, planning to peer if the entirety was proper enough, it might no longer have came about. That minute might have given you 10 extra minutes.

So what if you plan for 1/2-hour every day?

What you'll win the large image

If you advocate every day in solitude, on one hand, you'll keep away from errors. You'll take a look at beyond mistakes that you gained't repeat. Time gained. But as a substitute, you´ll see a manner to do the entirety quicker. More time gained.

Try it. Simply sit down down down correctly for your sofa for half of-hour in silence and also you´ll start to see possibilities to expand and expect to many barriers. You'll also discover who assist you to and wherein to discover the facts on the way to accelerate the entirety (it have come to be within the the front of you).

Yet regrettably maximum humans go away everything to danger. They live in an illusion of believing that the entirety gets higher inside the destiny. But just so they fool themselves. The proof is they constantly complain about lack of time.

And why does actually absolutely everyone fail in some component so critical as making plans? Because they suppose they already plan on the fly. They assume all day lengthy! While they art work… While they devour... But this isn´t making plans. This is intellectual noise. To really get consequences you need to isolate yourself in silence. Alone.

Yet most humans, after they have a few unfastened time, they choose out to relaxation. They deserve it! And they play with their cellular in desire to wondering for 10 minutes. Perfect, it´s their right. There also are others so crushed through the usage of their every day, that they truly count on they don´t have time to devise. What they do is sincerely too critical to prevent and count on. Perfect, it´s their right furthermore. But none of them will collect their goals inside the event that they do not isolate time to assume.

The risk of now not making plans

I knew a salesman who continuously were given out of area in infinite consumer necessities and technical specifications. He labored difficult, however in his marketing campaign to be the hero, he lost masses of hours in long opinions and infinite technical discussions. Even with clients who hardly ever sold.

"You can't leave the patron on my own," he stated to shield himself. And his profits, of course, went down. Did the salesclerk artwork difficult? Yes, but he did not reputation on the huge goals.

Because he failed to plan. And as he did now not plan, he failed to get his priorities right. And so he persisted his warfare in opposition to evil. He persisted dropping his time -and the time of his coworkers- with extended opinions full of technicalities that weren´t a part of his job.

He ultimately were given fired. From that organisation and the following ones. Because he didn´t consciousness on priorities.

Lack of planning is also the principle reason of failure in managers. They grow to be specializing in the incorrect dreams. They even do obligations that have to be delegated. It´s the hero syndrome. Trying to clear up the entirety. It´s like while a income supervisor currently suggested me that his earnings had been lowering notwithstanding he for my part managed many customers. Yet how should he sell greater if he changed into dropping his time touring customers, as opposed to planning strategies collectively along with his salesmen? How may want to he sell more if he didn´t examine deviations and layout gives?

I advised him he become doing incorrect. "Stop making noise," I stated to him right away. He didn´t love it. But he modified into smart and changed his technique. He became skilled and knew the marketplace, but this would not serve him if he did no longer recognition at the 3 vital points. So he changed his method and sat down for two weeks first-rate to plot. Immediately his sales stopped reducing. And while he noticed the ones first outcomes he endured planning extra and delegating all he have to. And his income persisted growing.

On the opportunity hand, I moreover met a monetary director who didn´t plan and so he didn´t cognizance on negotiating the credit score score conditions with the banks. And that way his corporation misplaced coins. The director grow to be a nice individual and his group cherished him, but he in no manner seriously planned his actual goals. And because of the reality he didn't isolate time to suppose, he did no longer consciousness on the real priorities. Finally he end up fired.

That's why whether or not you are an worker or have your very personal organization, you ought to plan. The advantages are terrific. Because there´s continuously something so one can make you grow faster. And sincerely with the beneficial aid of thinking about it, you´ll discover the answer.

So you need to behave much less and suppose extra. Even if you anticipate you do now not have time to devise. Because even ten minutes an afternoon of making plans should save you a every day hour of extra artwork. Isn't it clearly surely worth it?

All the time you spend wondering will multiply your rewards. Seriously, attempt it. After studying this, isolate 1/2 of-hour to check your scenario and you will see super possibilities. Only half-hour. The solutions had been already there. But you'll in no way have located them with out preventing and thinking.

So whilst you concentrate your self announcing, "I even have a lot to do this I cannot prevent to assume," you're in chance. Or even as you are saying, "I become too tired after paintings to anticipate greater." Or on the identical time as you say, "Whenever I attempt to devise, an urgency seems." These mind are a entice. Because nothing is more critical than planning. So set apart half of an hour each day to plot and you´ll start to remedy the chaos that now limits you.

And in case you do now not have half-hour to suppose?

Then set apart hours.

Do you've got time for everything?

One query, do you believe you studied you do not have time to acquire your real desires?

You have time.

You have time for what's important. Remember that point you had an not possible situation but pulled out forces from nothing? You made it due to the fact you focused on it. And you centered on it due to the reality you deliberate it. Strength comes after readability. It´s the number one advantage of making plans. Seeing you've got got time for the important things.

I apprehend what you're wondering now. Currently you've got extra pending duties than you can give up. This demoralizes you and produces indiscipline. But this could opposite when you plan. Because you´ll revise the whole lot. For what venture would possibly you give up many exclusive duties? Which are the real books you need to examine? What are you able to do without?

When you intend, the large revelation will seem: are the responsibilities you considered critical, simply crucial? And so that you'll take away loads of vain duties that eat your existence.

So in no manner fall into the trap of thinking that even as you intend you do no longer paintings. Quite the opposite.

You are saving time.

You're attracting your desires. You're putting off what can move wrong. You're preventing someone from stabbing you inside the lower back. You're already winning.

So set aside half of an hour a day to expect. It can be additionally snug. Lying for your couch even as you progress for your dreams. Yet the high-quality detail is that you'll have revelation after revelation. And while you discover ways to collect your goals lots faster, you will need to maintain going. Because you can see that 20% of what you do gives you 80% of results. And so you´ll increase that 20%.

And now the query is, how do you begin planning? How do you get results speedy?

How to get commenced out: three Tips

Don't worry if you do no longer realize a manner to start your new strategist life. No one emerge as born planning properly. So proper right here are three factors to help you to look outcomes fast.

1. Start via constructing for your strengths

When you begin making plans you´ll be so overloaded with responsibilities which you could now not recognize wherein to begin. So truly ask your self: what obligations deliver me maximum of the profits right now?

When doubtful, start studying your consequences. Or better stated, consciousness on what gives you the maximum crucial advantage and make it large. So ask your self what products or services should your clients pay greater for? Find it first. Whether you've got were given your private business enterprise or art work for a organisation, commonly help your electricity. You want a guide.

And therefore study Pareto´s Law. There´s always a 20% as a manner to provide you with 80% outcomes. It always works: 20% of your moves provide you with 80% of your profits. Which technique that 80% of what you do high-quality gives you 20% of results! So stumble on your golden 20% and from there make the awesome plans.

Imagine as an instance you figure in income. Your key is locating new clients and designing suitable gives. And the relaxation? Eliminate it ruthlessly. It might be tempting to resolve technical problems. It may be comfortable to do customer service (mainly with clients you want incredible). But you have to popularity on most income. And meaning getting rid of some thing that does not belong to the golden 20% that gives you eighty% of turnover. If crucial, communicate it over along side your superiors. Make them see they may earn more so. And if they insist to art work on other responsibilities, you aren´t inside the proper enterprise. Priceless data.

The same in case you lead a collection or a employer. What's your 20/eighty? It can be probably motivating your institution, reading deviations, and checking that the whole lot receives completed on time. The rest will pleasant harm you.

So start planning proper via focusing for your key component. What´s already offering you with income and you may growth? From there the extremely good techniques will emerge.

Every case is extremely good, however you´ll commonly do properly if you guide your sturdy element and take away tempting secondary obligations no longer associated with your number one cause. Otherwise you´ll lose your profession extinguishing fires and counting on a paycheck that allows you to infrequently growth.

2. Don't obsess approximately even as

The question many ask while leaping to the wondering extra way of life is: but on the identical time as to do it? Is there a wonderful time?

The answer is easy: plan whenever you could. Your mind is extra energizing first time inside the morning. It's the excellent period for everything. For planning however moreover to cognizance on your maximum critical mission. Between 7:00 a.M. And 9:00 a.M. Is your brightest time. But in case you're comfortable getting important tasks completed early inside the morning, plan later. It's approximately doing it, not at the equal time as to do it.

So do now not overcomplicate matters. It's additionally ok to plot at noon, or on the quit of the day. Important is which you count on calmly. It does not recollect if you take a seat down or lie down. Yet avoid interruptions. No documents to check. No Internet. But with paper and pen to install writing thoughts and timelines.

The advantages of the primary hour

Planning early in the morning is outstanding, you´ll be more lucid. But you furthermore mght need this period to attack important stuff. So it´s nevertheless legitimate putting your wondering time later. Especially information you completed the critical work of the day.

The key's that you don´t waste your first hours studying emails or in conferences. If you start the day with B obligations, you´ll come to be with B duties. Because unproductive matters multiply. From one unimportant difficulty you jump to each exceptional extra unimportant. And then any other and some one-of-a-kind... You ought to maintain for a life-time so.

So anyways use your first hour for some aspect vital, no matter if it´s planning or jogging to your primary mission. It´s important to growth a robust electricity of will.

three. Isolate at the least 1/2-hour for making plans.

And how a bargain time must you spend thinking?

To start goal for 30 minutes. Plan 1/2 of an hour each day and in a few days you´ll see such a lot of advantages which you´ll increase that point.

But crucial: do it in a unmarried move. Don´t interrupt your wondering time to complete a few pressing assignment. Nothing is more pressing than questioning. And take care due to the fact you´ll continuously be tempted to perform a little factor else. Yet excellent conclusions nice come after non-prevent questioning. Only even as you immerse your self in a few aspect deep, properly thoughts will come. They don´t seem after five minutes, the splendid explosion starts offevolved after 20 mins, as quickly as your thoughts is aware of you´re critical about it.

Follow the above 3 keys and you´ll make the quality plans. And now right right here are eight greater pointers to plot like a hold close and attain all of your dreams.

8 Keys to area your self and attain your dreams

If you need fast results, planning is essential. And right right right here are 8 more ideas to do it. Any of them may be the key to boosting your results.

KEY 1: First the 20/80

Time is limited and also you can't wander off in responsibilities that go nowhere. And consequently undergo in thoughts: recognition best on your strengths. What 20% offers you 80% of your income? This need to be your applicable concept whilst planning. Always orientated to boom.

What task will make you development quicker?

KEY 2: Understand that the answer is already on your head

The option to any trouble already exists. But you want to assume in solitude to find out it out.

You already have the entirety you want inner. Think for example about that venture this is taking longer than you notion. You are crushed and desperately want to finish it. So save you making an funding greater hours!

And anticipate.

Isolate one targeted hour to appearance how you may do better. You´ll undo numerous knots, consider me. Maybe you´ll see that in case you reward yourself for every improve, you´ll boost up the approach. Or perhaps you´ll don't forget a e-book with a way to help you. In any case, you´ll stand up at the least with or 3 thoughts an first-rate manner to hurry up your task. Because take into account: questioning gives you 10X that factor. Look at it as a exchange-off. To win you need to deliver first. And your way of giving is thinking. Only then your advanced mind will respond revealing the solutions.

KEY three: Spend the primary two making plans minutes revising your next day

To get going speedy, start planning your next day. It´s fine two minutes. Simply ask yourself: what is going to you do the next day from 8.00 to 10.00, from 10.00 to 12.00, from 12.00 to fourteen.00, etc.? Divide your day in chunks of time and also you´ll be aware without delay how your brain wakes up and exquisite thoughts emerge.

Beginning is the critical component. And it´s as smooth as designing your next day. Start with the short time period and the large lines will emerge. As mins bypass, greater thoughts will seem.

Note: Try moreover to revise your subsequent day for one minute earlier than going to sleep. Your subconscious thoughts will keep running for you at some stage in the night time time and subsequent morning you may wake up complete of appropriate thoughts and electricity.

KEY four: Break it down, damage it down, and destroy it down all over again

When planning, spoil down every motive into the detail. The extra records, the easier your actions.

Once you have easy goals, you discovered the manner to do it within the first part of this financial wreck, damage them down into sub-desires. Design the records of that method, that verbal exchange, or that product. The smaller the factors, the quicker you´ll accomplish them.

KEY five: Recalculate times

This is vital. Understand that the entirety takes three times longer than you predicted the number one time.

We are too optimistic in our first calculation. In the preliminary euphoria, plans and greater plans emerge. A real orgy of well intentions. But then comes fact and the entirety takes three times longer than anticipated.

 Check it out. How a tremendous deal time did your very last challenge absolutely take? How a outstanding deal time doing the ones cellular telephone calls? It took typically 3 times greater than predicted. It´s regular. Don´t panic. We normally have a propensity to devise too with a bit of success at the start. That's why you want to recalculate it sluggish, moreover referred to as recognizing it'll take three instances longer. Essential not to surrender later.

Also add 30 more mins on every occasion you intend a change of project. It´s what your mind desires to exchange to a modern-day project.

KEY 6: What can bypass incorrect?

Negativity is first rate for planning.

If you want to be on time for a key meeting, anticipate unplanned visitors. If you want to coordinate a task, anticipate that a person out of your institution will fail. Stay cool and recall what might also moreover bypass wrong.

One of the brilliant advantages of planning is foreseeing boundaries. That's why negativity is proper for planning. This does now not suggest being terrible, this suggests being smart and searching beforehand to. For example, what ought to flow wrong to your subsequent negotiation? What may want to you are saying then? And at the same time... How will the opportunity facet counterattack?

If you count on, you win. The extra you reflect onconsideration on setbacks, the less setbacks you'll have. It's just a few minutes a good way to give you wonderful effects. As army strategist Sun Tzu said, "Victorious warriors win first after which go to struggle."

KEY 7: Avoid this mistake

Be cautious because of the fact whilst planning you'll be tempted to straight away try the thoughts you have got were given. It might be also easy to check statistics. But this may lead you to check greater statistics... That will lead you to every different micro venture... That will lead you to test greater statistics... Dangerous!

Your movements after planning might be amazing. But usually after planning. Don´t ruin your golden time. When questioning top notch you and a paper to write down ideas.

KEY 8: Enlarge your thinking time. Make your team plan

Why not multiply your results way to others´ thoughts? So inspire your organization and buddies to plan. Don't be tempted to be the celebrity that solves the whole thing.

Let others be brighter than you. And praise them for their mind. If you don´t have coins, a first-rate reward is congratulating them publicly. People love to be identified. They win and also you win.

You do no longer want the proper plan

It´s infinite what you could´t achieve with the useful aid of planning. Every minute you make investments thinking pays you commonly lower back. Yet the query is, do you need therefore a honestly excellent plan?

No. If you actually look into the destiny and foresee what can pass incorrect, you´ll make tremendous plans. You´ll see many opportunities and store time.

The sky's the limit in case you plan. Do you need your first-rate way of existence now? If you propose it´s feasible. You pleasant need to sit down and assume. What can pass wrong? Only this can push you instead.

One of the benefits of making plans is that, even in case your plan isn't best, you can make tremendous actions. And the self-control to withstand temptations may also seem. And of route... You´ll do away with needless obligations so that you can offer you with extra time. So in case you start making plans these days, in reality start thru reading your state of affairs. What are the key factors that cannot cross incorrect? How to make investments more time in what´s important and cast off secondary obligations?

First is having your dreams smooth, as you observed before, and then breaking them down. And in case you do not know your large purpose, without a doubt start making plans your next day. How are you able to reorganize your office to start day after today at whole tempo? How to barter that reduce rate? How to set up the subsequent occasion to make it a fulfillment? And severa ideas will come.

And in case you aren´t now in your ideal interest?

Maybe due to the fact you aren´t for your dream method now you trust you studied you do no longer want to devise. Once topics pass better, you can layout extremely good techniques!

But begin now. Train your self. Organize priorities, visualize results, and save you barriers. You´ll find out it impossible to resist. And it'll moreover let you accumulate your dream venture quicker.

The extra you advise, the earlier the destiny will come. If although doubtful, reflect onconsideration on what your lifestyles could be like now if you had deliberate extra. The remorse of no longer having idea to obtain extra desires may be painful. But it will push you to begin. So begin these days writing your dreams and then genuinely remember what you may do day after today. Because it is not too late. If you begin planning nowadays, things will alternate speedy.